On the Move

A guide to fruitful long term travelling and immigration based on psychology and a smile

Lars K. Hansen, MRCPsych, MD
Consultant Psychiatrist,
Wootton Cottage, Knightwood Close
Lyndhurst SO43 7DR, UK

"To change carries risks, but to stand still is fatal".

John Harvey Jones

New Generation **Publishing**

Index

Preface

"Life is elsewhere".
Rebelais

I have really been looking forward to writing this book. Pinning down at least some of all the thoughts and emotions that have been swirling around unnamed in my head over the last many years in exile seemed to have become a prerogative. From my daytime job as a psychiatrist I am well aware of the importance of articulating difficult thoughts and emotions. The consequence of not doing so may cause all sorts of problems for yourself and – not to forget – people around you.

The act of leaving your native country and attempting to live in a new and invariably different culture is a process that people of the modern world experience more and more frequently, especially the young. Within Europe the free movement of work force has created hitherto unprecedented levels of migration between the countries. Seen from the outside Fortress Europe may seem impenetrable, but one only has to walk down any modern, big-city street to convince oneself that that is a truth with modifications. Throughout history of mankind people have moved away to seek greener pastures and perhaps also to seek out other, less tangible objectives. Seneca said: "However far we go, it is only to meet ourselves at the end of the journey."

Before we get as far as the end of the journey there are lots of people to meet and situations to tackle.

Emigrate – why?

On the surface, there can be many ways in which people try to justify their embarkation on the arduous journey of traveling and settling down elsewhere.

Most will recognize probably one or a combination of the following reasons:

- love
- seeking status
- financial reasons or academic/artistic ambitions
- urge for newness/restlessness
- ruthlessness/hate
- de facto suicide
- moral conviction
- against their will (forced exile)
- hopes of freedom
- critical incidents
- simply a wish for a better life, unspecified
- in search of a challenge because life is good
- Anger and frustration are other, often neglected, reasons for immigration.

We shall have a closer look at the motivations for leaving in chapter one.

You will get rich!

Furthermore, this book will be exploring some of the enormous gains and potential pitfalls involved in moving away from, and eventually returning to, your home territory. The main focus will be on immigration based on free choice. The book is among other things an attempt to share some of my private experiences and mistakes on foreign shores, hopefully capturing the universal in the personal. In other words, it is a guide book to a more meaningful integration wherever it may take place. Integration does not only happen when you have left your country and attempt to settle elsewhere, it happens whenever you are confronted with a culture thus far unknown to you. This may be as mundane as starting in a new work place, starting a new school or maybe visiting your in-laws. More or less the same process and more or less the same universal rules and regulations of integration apply.

My personal experience of leaving my native Denmark for a mixture of love, academic ambition and search for newness – that unfortunately quickly turned into merely academic ambition and search for novelty – has naturally colored the content of this book greatly.

There certainly have been moments, some of them extremely long, where I have questioned my own sanity for continuing Project Emigration/Immigration. But the meeting of the New World (the new, unfamiliar country and all of the indigenous people) and the Old World (represented by the frail and lonely you) does in the longer term give you a stronger sense of who you are and what you would like to do with the rest of your life. The energy created from this meeting of different worlds is bound to influence you for life and put many other challenges into appropriate perspective. Our skills to "pick and mix" from the cultural meeting are put to the test. All in all, immigration is an unrivalled learning opportunity that, no matter what happens, will leave you as a richer and more insightful person. Journeys are known to be the midwives of thought.

Chapter I

Why we leave

> *"A man must carry knowledge with him, if he wants to bring knowledge home."*
> Samuel Johnson

Power of envy

"Could I be of any assistance?"I heard a boy of my age (15) say to two American girls of similar age. Until that moment the boy had, in my eyes, been a very ordinary boy that I had met at tennis tournaments on a couple of occasions over the previous years. He was not an outstanding player, he had no particular physical characteristics that made him stand out, he was all in all not a person that I noticed much at all. And there he was, suddenly transformed into a knight in shining armour rescuing trembling maidens from the ignorance of the bewildered, Danish ice cream man who did not speak a word of English. He swung his sword of flawless American English with lightning efficacy. The girls blushed suitably but were not coy in expressing their gratitude to the gallant stranger. I was truly flabbergasted and in awe of the boy's ability to change language at the spur of the moment. The ice cream man was happy that another deal was sealed, the girls were dazzled, and I was influenced for life.

This little incident took place outside an ice cream van in the early eighties behind an utterly forgettable tennis club in Copenhagen suburbia. I spent the rest of the tournament attempting to piece together what was behind the boy's talent for the metamorphosis that I had accidentally witnessed. It turned out that he was the son of an American man living in Denmark. The language at home was English, which in itself was fascinating for a boy like me from the Danish countryside. The boy explained to me that he sometimes used his language skills as a hidden talisman if in trouble.

He would scream and use some of the worst swear words he knew in English if cornered by Danish bullies, he would play the innocent foreigner when caught on the train without a ticket, and would always be able to placate his father's anger by speaking to him in his mother tongue. Worst of all, he was, despite his tender age, already fully aware of the effect on the opposite sex of his status as an exotic fruit.

I wanted to be as exotic as he. But that was difficult, being Danish, living in the Danish sticks, going to a Danish school. In my youthful naivety I soon came to the conclusion that only emigration would catapult me into the wanted state of affairs in one swoop. I believe that my vagrant lifestyle was partially decided on that summer's day in 1980.

Party pooper

It is nevertheless far from clear why some people get up and leave and others decide to stick it out where they are. It is quite similar to a late night party where some choose to stay because they believe this particular party has what it takes to keep them, be it alcohol, attractive potential sex partners, the right kind of music etc. This may be because the stayers are fearful of trading in what they have for the unknown, or perhaps because they are worried of causing offence to the host or perhaps because they do not have the curiosity to imagine a world different from the one they are seeing there and then. Others may feel that it is time for them to leave for a nightclub because they are not satisfied with what the party can offer.

"Stay. Together we can change the music and we will buy some different wine" might be the first group's argument to try to persuade the restless to stay. Minor adjustments like these would have sufficient impact on some, usually the majority, to acquiesce and stay.

But still, a small group of seriously restless partygoers would remain determined to leave regardless of any attempts of persuasion.

The simple fact that somebody is leaving the party will inevitably force the remaining group to ask questions, initially directed at the party-leavers, later at themselves. Leaving is therefore an act of treachery as it threatens the status quo of any group. Just ask the heretics during the inquisition about that! It obviously angers the people left behind when their argument seems to be ignored by the restless. They may as a last attempt, in a fit of ill-concealed, aggrieved narcissism, try to accuse the leavers that they are dodging an unwritten set of rules and responsibility towards the party: "You accepted the invitation and now you are simply quitting because it suits you".

This is hard-hitting stuff that strongly implies a sense of betrayal. This will drain the resolve from yet more of the people who initially set out to leave. Only a very hard core will actually defy all the natural fears of the unknown combined with powerful heckling from the people left behind, and still get up and go.

But if just one single person leaves it will automatically make the group that stayed behind wonder about the quality of life they are having. They may try to minimize the loss by denouncing the leaver as an irresponsible quitter that was never worth much anyway, as a renegade that has transgressed the traditional rules of community spirit. But the damage has been done and the belief in the stayers' own life been shaken.

Many modern immigrants recognize the situation where people from the Old World appear to have little understanding for the need for change. It may very well be because the stayers see no good reason for change in their lives. It may also be because they fail to pluck up the courage to do something about their own situation. It is therefore more comfortable to resent the emigrant than questioning themselves for lack of initiative. The people that stayed behind may also secretly admire the emigrants' bravery without wanting to stir up turmoil in their own lives. This is clearly a common reason for strained relationships between the emigrant and the old world.

A now deceased family member of mine, petrified of losing his way, once advised me never to go anywhere for the first time!

Traitor

Emigrating is in many ways not unlike breaking up from a long term relationship; a sense of low key discontent and chronic annoyance with issues that seem as stagnant as brackish water in a pond, and perhaps intoxicatingly combined with having had an exotic whiff of the joys of foreign shores. You are convinced that you must go while you can, but how do you break the news without breaking hearts? You cannot.

Often, a strong feeling of betrayal becomes a nagging companion for the emigrant. The eyes of your ex-lover seething with disgruntlement seem to follow you everywhere you go. Forgiveness is not on the cards. How can you leave behind the lover who has given you so much; your identity, your culture, your language, your history, your understanding, even your life? Or so it appears at the time of departure.

It tears you apart. But in your heart you know you must do it. No matter what. Safety by inertia is not an option; it would be rather like death by default. You feel you must leave the old, reliable, sacrificing devotee for a fresh, virginal lover so full of excitement, so full of new hope, but oh, so short on promises.

Causing tears
Choosing the moment to open the discussion takes all the tact in the world. It depends on individual circumstances but certain provisions generally help. Make sure there is time to discuss the subject at depth. Do not rush. Make sure your relatives get time to ask questions (usually, "is it my fault?"). Reassure them about the availability of modern, easy ways of communication and transport and about your continuous commitment to them and your relationship. And last but not least, reassure them that leaving does not mean you are not dying - quite the opposite.

However people react to you on announcing your decision to emigrate, it is bound to spark off longing – even before you are gone. And it works both ways. The sentimental, wistful look in your mother's eyes before you venture out on the obligatory rounds to bid farewell to all your friends and relatives is soul destroying. It becomes clearer in your mind what it must have been like emigrating 100 years ago, waving goodbye from a boat never to see your loved ones again. That is not the case now and there is every chance you will see each other again, either in the old or the new world. That does nevertheless not change the fact that it is one of the biggest decisions of your life to leave the old world and make a fresh start somewhere else. Decisions do not come much bigger than that and it takes the right amount of consideration; too little results in rashness, too much will stall the process. The balance is fine.

Uncertainty is human
The process of immigration has already begun long before leaving the old country. You attempt to prepare

yourselves emotionally by trying to focus on the conscious reasons behind the decision, again not unlike a relationship break-up. You may also try to focus on the negative sides of your present life in order to win the inner argument about "going or not going" that will still be raging in your mind long after the announcement of leaving has been made. Despite all attempts to convince yourself that you should be going, there will deep inside you be obstinate islands of objection to the whole project. Do not worry. Uncertainty is part of being human. Some of these "islands" will even reappear after years of immigration. This obstinacy can be forcibly experienced on waking up in the morning in the new world believing for a moment that you are still in the old world and that your mum is cooking breakfast, while in reality she may be so far away that she is actually cooking dinner for all you know. When reality hits you it gives you a sinking feeling, but it is survivable.

The argument will never be fully won or lost, not even after years of expatriate existence. An awareness of a certain price for the enterprise of emigration is always present in your mind. In times of early adversity in the new world the immigrant will inevitably, for longer or shorter periods, look back and think "why on earth did I do this?"

It should however remain your main objective to convince yourself that your reasons are valid enough to justify your decision to leave. This may be done by activating interesting, mental processes that we all use on a daily basis, by 'maximizing', 'minimizing' and public announcements.

The wavering individual can manage to obtain some level of certainty by maximizing selectively the good aspects of leaving (new opportunities, newness, pride of own courage) while minimizing the bad aspects (leaving known territory, loved ones, new uncertainties, etc). This is a normal way of dealing with inner conflicts that can be very helpful, especially when action is needed. It can nevertheless backfire drastically if these techniques are used to an extent where important factors are cast aside and minor points are allowed to play a disproportionate role in the decision process. A degree of balanced thinking is needed and best obtained by repeated discussions with valuable others.

Buying a ticket well in advance is a financial commitment that, along with stating your intent to go to friends and family, can also stiffen the resolve during last-second wavering. These are essentially the same techniques that ensure that married people are less likely to stray than cohabitants: the power of publicly stating your love and committing yourself financially makes backtracking less of an obvious option. You will come up against personal and interpersonal pressures to follow through on your commitment. Public commitments tend to be lasting commitments. By speaking up you are effectively handcuffing yourself to your decision.

The decision is taken and other, less mature coping strategies can be called upon to aid the beleaguered would-be emigrant; alcohol is a well tested way of numbing underlying conflicts – so is frantic sexual activity! In the terminal phase in the old world both methods are used extensively to overcome a spiraling insecurity about the whole project.

A more fruitful method is to write an extensive list of pros and cons and rate the importance of each item on an arbitrary scale from 0 – 100. Thereafter add up all the scores on each side which will leave you with a much better idea of whether your dissatisfaction with the status quo combined with the desirability of the proposed change outweighs the personal cost involved in changing. Do not, however, feel that the exercise has failed if you still do not feel one hundred percent sure. That is just being human.

The common reasons for leaving the old world were already summed up in the preface. It is appropriate to have a closer look at each of these reasons for why such groundbreaking decisions are made.

Love
Foreign fever

Young people of today in the developed world have rich opportunities to travel away on holiday, take part of their education or visit friends and family abroad. Travelling often remove the traditional values and ways of dealing with the world, resulting in unexpected amorous liaisons. Because of the intensity of these meetings – often enhanced by time pressure and other external restrictions – lasting effects can occur on the young, and not so young, mind, and with great rapidity turn into passionate love.

Safely back home again in the old world, planning of more permanent arrangements may start to take shape in the afflicted's mind in an enticing attempt to capture the elusive spirit of the holiday forever. The experience can be alluring. The intoxicating, "in-love" phase can become unnaturally long due to the absence of the reality provoking presence of the loved one.

Inter-cultural spark

Having said that, an intimate meeting between different cultures has an undeniable spark to it that can enrich the individual as well as the surrounding environment. If eventually you should decide to make the big move to join your loved-one in the new world, it furthermore provides you with a personal coach in the difficult game of reading unfamiliar cultural signals, - and on top of that, even a dedicated language teacher. If the new world partner at some stage wants to bother to learn your old world language you can take that as a very sure sign of commitment.

Local knowledge, such as how to get to the library, how to take the underground, suddenly becomes very valuable. Knowledge hitherto regarded as self-evident is now, puzzlingly, appreciated.

Tipping the power-balance

It must be clear that the power-balance between the lovers may be dramatically different when one of the two has taken the step and moved to the new partner's home land. Very suddenly the loved-one may be reduced from a fun-loving, confident holiday-maker to an insecure immigrant with similar levels of needs to that of a toddler; unable to fill in a form, find the supermarket and chat to friends in the new world language, among other things. Hopelessly hapless. This problem poses a sizeable challenge to most cross-boarder couples. Overcoming the vexations of early emigration together can on the other hand become the cement that keeps a relationship on track through rough times.

Seeking status

Most of us secretly hanker to be basking in the unlimited admiration of others. In the majority of societies it is perceived as a failure to be at the mercy of other people's judgment. Status seeking is therefore rarely openly acknowledged but nevertheless remains a crucially important factor in our activities. The fact is that we all, whether we like or not, remain enslaved to other people's thoughts of us and our actions.

Men of unsung standing can by migration emerge with a much improved public persona. The rewards of a higher social standing are considerable; attention, financial gain, improved sexual possibilities, larger margins for error and, not least, respect. These rewards are so desirable that travellers have been willing to go through life-threatening situations, or actually even lost their life, to achieve them. When David Livingstone, the Scottish explorer was greeted by the ambitious young American, H.M. Stanley with the famous words "Dr Livingstone, I presume", deep in the unexplored African continent, it is not unkind to contemplate that the noble rescuer was perhaps driven in some measure by hopes of the glory that would be bestowed on him on his return. He had gone through 236 days of untold hardships travelling through inhospitable and completed uncharted wilderness to find the white doctor and missionary in a village by Lake Tanganyika. In spite of serious fever attacks due to malaria contracted on this trip he continued to travel back to Africa to explore new areas for the rest of his life. He had a taste of what exploring could do for him and the way he was perceived.

Migrants leaving for this particular reason run a serious risk of disappointment. They can often feel stripped of the status they had in the community they left behind while being unable to climb the social ladder in the new world. Fortunately, status is not all it is cracked up to be; it is a concept much prone to adaptation, at least when the movement is upwards; "Mummy, Mummy, I want to be a policeman," says the little boy. Not long after the young man has achieved his life time dream of becoming a member of the force, he wants to become a police sergeant. If we are not careful, seeking status can become a never-ending treadmill. However, *loss* of status, especially if endured over a short span of time, can have a malignant effect to which it is altogether more difficult to adapt. Herein lays an important motivation for so-called homegrown terrorism.

Making an impression
The striving to be admired can also be targeted towards a specific group of people or a specific person. This person may be a loved one but may bizarrely also be a hated one. The desire to show this person that you can excel at schoolwork, sports or whatever it may be, can become so overwhelmingly strong that it approaches an obsession.

A significant person in your life may have mentioned at an impressionable moment that travelling or emigration would be valuable endeavours. Or they may indeed themselves have ventured out on such travels and thereby created a benchmark that you cannot refrain from trying to reach – or even beat.

It can be years down the line before you realize what an impact the benchmark-beating has had on your life. Sometimes this realisation never materialises. However, the striving to score points against the ghosts of the past may be partly useful. It creates a drive that may not necessarily have been there otherwise. A desire to better the way we are seen by others is frequently part of the baggage that the emigrant brings along with him to the new world, more often than not hidden away like a stowaway under other odds and ends.

Thus, it could appear as if human happiness is proportional to the number of people envying our position in society, though it is important to note that no evidence exist to suggest that people occupying the top positions in the hierarchy are significantly happier than those below them.

Ambitions

Since the infancy of mankind we have migrated to foreign lands to obtain better possibilities for survival. The exodus was commonly provoked by mortal enemies, overcrowding and disease or by failing food supplies – not unlike present day refugees from troubled countries. Many modern refugees claim asylum-seeker status in order to pursue the utterly human desire to improve their own, and their families', quality of life rather than fleeing from actual persecution in their homelands. The will to give oneself the most opportune conditions under which to live one's lives has been evolutionarily hardwired into our brains since the very earliest stages of life. Our remarkable success as a species is closely associated with this principle.

It is too hard

It is therefore not surprising that people from poorer countries have been flocking in great numbers to the richer western countries over the last decades. It is actually more surprising that the numbers have not been even greater. The limited numbers bear tribute to the tremendous effort required to uproot yourself, let alone a whole family, from your country of origin. How to deal with the current intake of people from poorer backgrounds is a controversial political question with no easy answers – though many have been suggested!

Merciless, international hierarchy

Poor immigrants are often viewed as a threat by certain fractions of the host-society. The poor immigrants arrive scared and even more sensitive than the average immigrant to the new world. The status of their home country in the merciless, international hierarchy of countries is built on the level of financial and technological development, and the general consensus opinion on the culture. If the position of his homeland was not understood by the migrant before he left the old world, a short spell in the new world will make this abundantly clear. If the old world culture, by the above mentioned crude standards, is deemed inferior, chances are that most of the migrants will either attempt to conform to the superior mainstream of the new world, or they will huddle together in ghettos with their own kind, now even more entrenched in their cultural beliefs than before they left.

Humiliation is a fertilizer

As human beings we always have an intuitive understanding of our place on both the local and the global, social ladder. The isolation of the immigrant ghetto from the surrounding society will almost inevitably lead to unopposed bitterness. This is fertile soil for ferocious hate, further alienation and even terrorism. It is the humiliated and excluded immigrant that will end up living up to the new world's most pessimistic expectations. It may be true that "roots are something trees have and that people have feet" (George Steiner), but when pushed, we will look for those elusive roots as if our lives depended on it.

I hasten to mention that this is not only a phenomenon seen in the western world but also in some of the poorest countries around the world in Africa and Asia, where immigrants are branded as inferior by their host countries. Had this issue been understood better, international terrorism may not have reached the scale it has today.

Emigration on first class

People from affluent, stable countries also emigrate. New research from the University of Copenhagen confirms that people with higher education from the developed world are more likely to travel and emigrate than people with lower education. Having a sense that emigration is a natural progression after having managed the available hurdles at home in the form of school, A-levels and then university, is not uncommon – seeking the ultimate graduation from what the academy of life has on offer. This particular migrant has become so used to look for new hurdles to overcome almost before he has finished was he was doing, that emigration seems like the most obvious of choices. Pushing back the frontiers of what at first seems impossible can become addictive, where cravings for new challenges occur as soon as things start to seem manageable.

These more privileged migrants typically explain to themselves and others that their move is about increasing their wealth, their knowledge or perhaps more opportune levels of stimulation. That may very well be the case, but arguably most moves have more to do with a more or less conscious desire for inner transformation than the above mentioned reasons. Psychoanalytical psychotherapy dismisses this desire as mere naivety; "you can't psychically move away from your demons". Or as Marilyn Monroe's biographer, Norman Mailer wrote: "One may as well suppose a law: if the past is full of old complications, the future will grow new ones."

That is thankfully not the whole truth.

Any significant geographical move is guaranteed to have a profound influence, not just superficially, but right to the core of the human soul, due to the pervasive nature of the experience. The old psychoanalysts were partly right that we cannot escape our inner demons entirely by embarking on long journeys. Some undeniable characteristics of our personality will remain relatively unaltered. But we can certainly expect fundamental cornerstones of the psyche such as confidence, sense of achievement and attitudes to self and others, to be changed during the course of an integration process.

History is full of examples of great artists having found their divine inspiration only after having escaped what they saw as the spiritual desert of their homelands. Picasso went to Paris, the Mann brothers to America, Karen Blixen to Africa, to find in themselves what they could not find at home. The irony is that their respective homelands have often been exploited as sources of inspiration by other artists on the run, which indicates that inspiration is less prodigal in the bosom of home and more prodigal in absence of home. History is however also full of people who went away with the same intentions of producing great art, and then failing to do so. Still, these unsuccessful artists found something in themselves abroad that they could not have found at home. The truth.

Whatever the aim of the migration is, whether we achieve what we set out to do or not, it will undoubtedly leave a lasting impact on the very building blocks that determine who we are as human beings.

Need for newness - restlessness
Baudelaire, 19-century French poet and boozer, cried out: "Anywhere, anywhere." He was hoping for some supernatural power to sweep him away from his northern French domicile and drop him off in an exotic corner of the world.

For him the height of the exotic was to be found in Egypt with its alien clothes, spicy foods not to mention, mystic, dark-eyed women. On his return from a trip to the land of his dreams the same author added less enthusiastically, but very insightfully that "Life is a hospital where every patient is obsessed by changing beds. This one wants to suffer in front of the radiator and that one thinks he would get better if he was by the window."

Reinvent yourself
Despite these words of warning, moving abroad is a unique opportunity for reinventing yourself. If you are not happy with the way you were, or the way other people perceived you, well, you can clear off and do it differently in a new world. Unknown to everyone in the new world, you can put on a new mask and become the person you always wanted to be. The new world is empoweringly memory-free. There is no risk of walking the streets that always made you feel numb, or running into stereotypical views of you as being as mediocre as they come. The adage that the problems remain the same (as mentioned above) no matter where you go is only true to some degree. The deeper seated themes are difficult to change (see Battle of Values), but even relatively ingrained traits can be modified after a brush with migration. It must however be stressed that is it advantageous to remain true to your core values and beliefs without being dogmatic about them.

As mentioned previously, the status quo is simply inconceivable when it comes to the human condition. Looking at other people, the would-be emigrant may argue that some people's lives appear to have stalled completely. At the early stages of the emigration process the eager emigrant becomes sensitive towards even the smallest sign of stagnation, in themselves as well as others. This obsession with stagnation is part of the self-persuasion process of staying on the emigration path and can easily become a trifle tiresome to innocent bystanders who may feel bombarded by critical remarks on how they conduct their lives.

Movement
But on closer examination, most people's lives are invariably in the process of movement, but not necessarily in the right direction. Some people get pleasure from the development of ever larger muscles, some by seeing their family expand, others by seeing their bank accounts grow steadily and still others – even more bizarrely – by increasing their share of problems. In any event, life is a moving process that, unaffected by attempts to obstruct the flow of changes, will move on with or without us. We do nevertheless have some degree of choice over the direction of flow.

As in any normal distribution, some people will show higher degree of desire for newness than other. The travel option is an optimal way to cater for that particular quest. It is possible to simultaneously harbour a strong urge for newness and what seems diametrically opposite, the desire for sameness. The point where the balance is poised between the two, goes a long way to define who you are as a human being.

The modern suffering of relative absence of torment in many privileged societies fuels the desire for newness for newness' sake. To some, the well-trodden path of going to work, returning home, going to bed etc. becomes intolerably mind numbing in spite of the fact that all the basic requirements seem amply fulfilled. The problem is that staying in your comfort zone will narrow down you life to an extent where even simple tasks become overwhelming. Longer stays in your comfort zone can give you the unpleasant feeling of the walls coming ever closer and finally crashing in on you. Comfort zones have a tendency to deliver surprisingly little genuine comfort for a place of that name. Samuel Beckett went as far as stating that habit is the power that chains the dog to its vomit.

You are in the grip of the opposite of homesickness. An often unarticulated urge to experience new things can become so overpowering that the individual has little other choice than to act on his impulses and change the direction of his or her life dramatically.

By emigrating you put yourself in a situation where the distance between sadness and joy, between good and bad fortune seem so much greater than in the old world. An enhanced sense that "something" could go terribly wrong - imagined or real - seems to guarantee an intensity of which the comfortable, old world life was so desperately devoid.

Baptism of fire

People that choose emigration to quell their desire for change may find it to be quite a baptism of fire - especially if the move follows years of relatively static life. Everything, from grocery-shopping to visits to the doctor, will possibly have to be dealt with in a foreign language and definitely in a different cultural climate. It is an immense challenge for which a previously sheltered life has not necessarily prepared you adequately. On the other hand, the benefits in form of human growth are enormous if you possess the streak of toughness it takes to convert frustration into fuel for perseverance. The human capacity for resilience in the face of challenges should never be underestimated, your own included. Seeing things as challenges instead of problems delineates the difference between inadequacy and growth.

Ruthlessness – hate

These two less chivalrous reasons for leaving the old world - because of the nature of the emotions – play an often unrecognized role in the mind of the emigrant. But in the minds of the people left behind in the old world, the negative reasons are often much more prominent because of feelings of rejection, being second-best and abandonment.

Hate is often related to an underlying feeling of shame. The origin of the shame can be culture-bound, from having had sex before marriage to somehow having failed to live up to expectations, or due to a range of other widely accepted misdemeanors. Casting shame on somebody is an excellent way of getting one's way. In some instances the basis of the shame may at this stage for the grown-up emigrant be rather nebulous, but still strong enough to be the major driving force behind the urge to get away from the humiliation. While hate has many parents, shame and humiliation only foster one child, hate.

Negative motivation

The nervous energy required to drive a person from his ancestral land quite commonly has its roots in deep seated disappointments and grievances. The covert motivation created by hate and resentment can be exceptionally forceful and make people bulldoze their way through seemingly impenetrable walls of troubles. If the underlying disharmonies have occurred during sensitive periods in someone's life, it may alter the person's perception of the world in the longer term. For these people the old world can appear as an unsafe and unwelcoming place. Dylan Thomas said about his old world, Wales "The land of my fathers… my fathers can have it!" And on this occasion he was reportedly not drunk.

We are mentally programmed to search for ways out of predicaments, and there is an obvious temptation to believe that everything would be better in a new world. That is why people go, only to find it is difficult to rid themselves of paranoid and hostile attitudes, even in a new environment. This is because a hostile attitude is amazingly self-confirmatory; if you arrive with a suspicious and aggressive attitude, you are, unless the company is unusually understanding and forgiving, almost certain to stir up reciprocal emotions. Of course this unfortunate turn of events is bound to ultimately confirm to those lacking insight that the new world is also full of unfriendly people.

For people with an abusive background, emigrating is seen as an effective technique of staying out of harm's way. The abuser may be long gone or insignificant in real terms to the adult person, but emigration may still be perceived as the only way of freeing him- or herself from the hated chains of the past. Similarly, excessive competition and rivalry, e.g. between siblings, can push people into emigration. The tearing of intimate ties can easily be construed as an act of ruthlessness by relatives in the old world, while for the emigrant it can feel more like the only way to carry on.

See it for what it is

These kinds of universal human reactions know no borders. Therefore emigration in itself cannot be recommended as a sole remedy for this problem, particularly given the fact that general suspiciousness will in any case rise for most individuals during the first period abroad. Some kind of 'peace agreement' with the old world is desirable before any definite travel plans are made. This can be done, not by having a more positive outlook, but rather by taking a more realistic view of things. Thereby a realisation should emerge that most worlds consist of – admittedly different - mixes of good and bad. If this realisation fails to materialise a tragic repeat performance is only too likely to take place on the greener grass of the new world.

De facto suicide
Another often overlooked reason for emigration is closely connected to the above mentioned motives to leave. Emigrating and leaving those people who are important to you, can be perceived as a de facto suicide, second only to the real thing. Emigration is a conscious attempt to remove yourself from the equation that has been your life hitherto. Some emigrants may get a thrill out of taking revenge by leaving, while others may have the disturbed view that going away can give the relatives a sense of relief that the black sheep of the family has gone away. Suicide researchers talk about an "altruistic suicide". Finally out of sight.

Left behind
It is not uncommon for feelings of horror, mourning, disbelief and resentment to grip the people left behind in the old world. These feelings only differ in degree from those of the real suicide victim. For the emigrant some hidden pleasure may consist in observing how much he is missed back home from the safe distance of the new world. The new world is a conveniently far away place to sit and sulk, a pleasure that real suicide victims to our knowledge do not have.

Role change

Leaving can be about shaking off an intolerable role that otherwise may have seemed inescapable. You may not be clear in your mind about what you want to be, but you do know that you do not want to be what you are now. The role may be, for example, about being seen to be boring, unlovable, morose, incapable, a crook, ridiculous or many other things. It may be about having being abused in the past and now finally being able to escape, in spite the fact that the original source of abuse is frequently no longer a threat. The abuse can cover many areas ranging from minor neglect to gross physical and sexual misdemeanors. What all those who have suffered have in common is that the abuse has made a lasting impression on them. By emigrating they have effectually exiled themselves into safety.

Emigration is an excellent way of committing a partial suicide. The hated role you once had will disappear – if you play your cards right - but you will live on. By leaving the old world you believe that you have cut out a cancerous lump of your past as with a stroke of surgical brilliance. But few treatments for cancer are curative and watchfulness is necessary in case of relapse. This role can be so despised it remains the main reason for why people cannot cope with returning home to the old world, even decades after they have left.

This analogy may be pushing it too far and most immigrants would not recognize this aspect of moving away. But if you do, attempting to understand exactly what it was that originally drove you away will be important for the future. If a hated role is one of your main reasons for leaving it must not be forgotten that real freedom is freedom without resentment. That kind of freedom is not easily obtainable unless some degree of forgiveness is involved. Not for the perpetrators sake, not for your sake, but for everybody's sake.

It is clear that certain cultures have a much higher level of internal acceptance of long-term travel than others. In these cultures it is possible that this reason for leaving has less relevance (e.g. New Zealand, as a result of being far away from everywhere else, and being originally a nation of emigrants). Nevertheless, some level of self-eradication – along with loads of self-edification - does take place in the process of leaving your country.

Just ask your relatives.

Moral conviction

Modern day travelling missionaries still exist. Some are very similar to those of earlier times, spreading the word of their preferred God, some are modern versions in form of politicians, school teachers, doctors and other aid-workers. All have the laudable intention of helping others in what these contemporary missionaries perceive as living under less fortunate conditions than themselves, be it financially or spiritually.

The majority of these "do-gooders" are genuinely sacrificing considerable personal benefits to help others without visible, ulterior motives. Abstaining from luxuriant life styles is not a new remedy for purging of the soul. Some of these people, just as some of the ones that leave for financial, academic or artistic purposes, are in one way or another frustrated by what they did at home in the old world. A virginal land is waiting to be taken by storm. There is nothing sinister about this motive for leaving. It only becomes sinister if the reasons below the surface are left uncovered.

If you have the courage to dig, you may be rewarded with treasures of information about you and your world, old as well as new.

Addicted

Regardless of the motivation, many of these people do a marvelous job far beyond the call of duty. Some left their old-world partly to fill minor gaps in their own lives, only to find that filling major holes in others' lives becomes a calling. This can become all engulfing and for a number of people it becomes a life-long obsession. The gratitude in the eyes of the less fortunate is addictive and the hard-hitting suffering can make the return to a pampered life in the industrialized world difficult. The problems of the rich world can seem so utterly trite after experiencing how quickly life can be exchanged for death in worlds seemingly far away. The sense of making a real difference is not easy to replicate behind a privet hedge back in the old world.

It is peculiar how making a difference for others can negate the fundamental absurdity of life... and how that absurdity will shine even brighter if we are deprived of making that difference. No one knows this better than people who have traveled with moral conviction.

Forced exile

The Greek philosopher Epictetus once said that anywhere is a prison if you do not want to be there. An increasing number of people, mainly from the poorer countries of the world, attempt to escape intolerable conditions and perhaps even persecution. How to deal with these vagabonds of global migrations, so called economic migrants, now arriving on a hitherto unknown scale has become a political conundrum for richer societies.

The rising numbers are caused not by increased suffering in the world, but by a combination of improvements in the global infrastructure (airplanes, cars, road etc.), by more uniform hopes for the future and simply by the fact that there are more of us now than ever before in history.

The forced exile deprives people of feeling that they have a say in the matter, spat out of their home country like unwanted grape seeds. Psychological research has repeatedly pointed out that a sense of internal locus of control over our own destiny is pivotal in creating a sense of well being. These people usually have a distinct sense of an *external* locus of control. In addition to this, poor newcomers in the richer host country are often met with a pervasive enmity and antagonism – sometimes overt, sometimes subtle, but nevertheless damaging.

Forming groups
Shying away from others that look or behave noticeably differently from ourselves is, unfortunately, an integral part of the human make-up and how we form groups. In particular, if we sense that no immediate advantage can be gained from knowing the newcomer, attitudes can rapidly become less than welcoming. This is neither evil nor psychopathic but simply a product of our millennia old, evolutionary background where these traits increased our chances of survival by strengthening the sense of belonging to one group and ensuring that the group did not lose power by admitting weaker members.

People who loudly announce that they embrace all different cultures with equal enthusiasm not uncommonly have a hidden agenda. Encouraging 'differentness' can, in their group, be seen as "cool" and therefore enhances the status of those who champion that particular view. The proactive enthusiasm may therefore have more to do with the person's own schema than with serious attempts to breed integration.

Minor differences can in some instances be accepted and indeed be seen as enticing and exotic by many. While major differences come across as unbecoming, cumbersome and even threatening. The level of 'differentness' with which you can cope is usually directly linked to how secure you are in yourself, both at a personal and financial level. Time and again over the last decade, the 'little man' in the western societies has protested with mounting anger about the growing numbers of immigrants. The weaker classes of a society feel overrun and disempowered perhaps because they regard their own situation as precarious. This has happened in most western European countries, Germany, France, Italy, but also in traditional immigrant-countries as New Zealand, Australia and the USA. These protests have in certain countries resulted in the growth of political parties whose primary function has been to voice the dissent of these people.

The higher the number of immigrants, the more momentum these organized protests will gather. Any society has a saturation point, and some would argue that where it is pitched is a direct reflection of that society's level of civilization and maturity. Milan Kundera writes beautifully that "true human goodness, in all its purity and freedom, can come to the fore only when it recipient has no power. Mankind's true moral test, its fundamental test, consists in its attitude towards those who are at its mercy." Kundera was talking about animals, but he might as well have been talking about immigrants. It now looks increasing likely that the rich countries, in response to public demands for a tightening of immigration laws, will establish an individual (i.e. less permissive) interpretation of the original Geneva-convention of 1951 regarding refugees. It is a political decision how big the holes in the immigration net ought to be.

Exploitation of desperation

However, bypassing the net altogether poses a risk both to host and to immigrants. Human smugglers and organized gangster organizations have become progressively more ingenious in running rings around the police, thereby raising the numbers of illegal immigrants in some of the most sought-after western societies. Such organizations represent the lowest of the low: Exploitation of desperation. This leaves the public in the host countries with the impression that immigration is effectively out of control. The market in human smuggling is lucrative and of course at the expense of the host society (and actually, of the donor country too), not to mention the fact that some migrants commonly have to pay absurd amounts of money for a ticket to a country of which in many cases they know little or nothing . The illegal trade in human misery puts the migrants at acute risk in more ways than one. Not only do they sometimes have to deal with life-threatening travel conditions before they reach their destination, but they also, on arrival, risk further discriminatory and vigilante-style treatment from agitated subgroups within the host nation.

This is by no means a behaviour confined to privileged westerners feeling threatened on their colour TV and on their yearly outing to Ibiza, but is also a pattern seen in and around refugee camps in the most desolate areas of the world. 'Differentness' is perceived as a threat in most societies – and indeed it is, to the status quo… which is an illusion anyway. The pace with which societies change is only partly controllable by political means. That pace of change has undoubtedly increased over the last decade in no small way thanks to mass immigration.

Adapt or die

For the individual caught up in this web of difficulties it is crucial for him to preserve his personal dignity and not be weighed down by bitterness. If bitterness prevails it effectively prevents adaptation to the new environment from taking place, and the battle is lost before it has begun. Adaptation is essential for 'successful' immigration. Adaptation, not at any price, not wholly on others' terms, but on your terms too. Adaptation at any price is not adaptation, it is 'copying', a largely worthless exercise. Unquestioning allegiance to a cause or to a new identity is always bad news. Along with bitterness, copying is probably the most important pitfall to avoid for the shell-shocked newcomer forced to flee his homeland. I have seen good people, especially from nations which see themselves as inferior, engage in the humiliating process of kowtowing and obsequious copying of what they perceive to be the 'gold standard' persona of the new world . They emphasise their new identity in a bid to reject their past. Ingratiating themselves to the indifferent (at best) 'new worlders' becomes a priority – not unlike the way a cat rubs itself against the legs of its master. Just more nauseating. Copying behaviour is driven by the abiding urge of the shipwrecked soul to belong. The urge becomes even more acute when embarrassed about the ties to the old world. The little joke, the twinkle in the eye is carefully avoided not to break any new world rules – rules that often do not even exist.

The copycats will go to extremes to be as indistinguishable as possible from the culture of the new world, by adopting its clothes, after shave, music, tastes, interests, accents, partners etc. And despite all these efforts they will never succeed.

The Englishman DH Lawrence wrote of America some 80 years ago: "You cannot have a new thing without breaking an old". This is the flawed mantra of the copycats who refuse to recognize and honour their past. All too often have I innocently asked people where they were from originally, and have been met with a "Why?" said with a mixture of suspicion, anger and fear. Suspicion because they worried about being prejudged, anger because they have been "found out" not to be from the new world, fear because they feel unsure of what the consequences of this discovery will be.

But we cannot be whole without our past, in which are invested our memories, pride and sense of right and wrong. Integration is about adding new aspects to your personality while copying is a detraction process. It is not a choice between the new and the old world - in fact, we must choose both. Adaptation and integration is a constant negotiation with your surroundings. Without it, all is lost - with it, we have all won.

Critical incidents

It is not uncommon that emigrants have experienced in their recent past some sort of momentous incident in the lead-up to departure. It is as if the incident that took place was precisely what it took to jolt them into 'unfreeze' mode. Suddenly it seemed crystal clear that current practices were no longer good enough to satisfy the unfrozen mind.

The emigrant influenced by such events may find it difficult to comprehend that he did not see things in the same perspective before the incident.

The incidents may be positive (marriage, sudden wealth, passed exams) but more often than not, it is an negative event, such as relationship rupture, disease, death in the family, loss of assets, accidents etc. that sets the mind on a mission to change. This source of energy can be very strong and is unlikely to be stopped easily. The blinkers have been forced off and the world suddenly looks very different.

Emigrants that have gone through shattering experiences are advised to proceed with care and take a little time to rethink, otherwise new storms may be brewing ahead. But again, the balance is delicate. Waiting too long can mean that the momentum is lost, and with that, the chance to step out of yourself.

The wish for a better life

"I want to live in the sun" is an argument that is often heard in more northern parts of the northern hemisphere. Climate is commonly linked to lifestyle and opportunities. Few things can make the northerner more wistful than images of sun-drenched beaches full of relaxed people having fun. It is as if they expect that a statutory link between happiness and sun exists. Even though many aspects of our existence are undoubtedly positively influenced by a pleasant climate, the link is as capricious as April weather in northern Europe. We ignore that at our peril.

The wish for a better life is born out of a nagging fear of life passing you by without you being in the midst of the action. Simultaneously, emigrants harboring this reason for leaving are driven by an uneasy sense that they are constrained by comfortable certainty. Routines and everyday life tend to blunt sensibilities.

Keeping awake

Nothing awakes you more from the eternal slumber of everyday life than travelling. Newly found mobility offers an imaginative counterweight to feelings of stagnation and confinement. A wonderful resurgence of curiosity and alertness can be experienced. Things are experienced with a renewed appetite for life, with the wonder of small child that sees the world for the first time. It is a tonic with boundless powers to shake you out of hibernation. But unfortunately, no tonic without side effects. These can be a proportionate resurgence in paranoia, homesickness, loss of confidence, accompanied by the inability to switch back to 'cruise control' when exhausted.

Yet, it works. Migration brings men which decades before died the death of routines and pettiness back to life, because they have to. Travelling, and migration in particular, is life without the wrapping. You are in certain ways confronted with a 'do or die' situation that will make you live your life more acutely. With no more unknown continents to conquer, emigration is the modern equivalent of the adventures of earlier days' explorers. The scene is artificial and the risk of getting eaten alive by savages only remote, but it is undoubtedly the same psychological mechanisms at play which forced Cook and Columbus on their way into unknown territories.

Travel genes

Modern man usually has some idea from media, books, verbal reports or even accounts of previous travels about the country where he is heading, which was rarely the case for the old explorers. The notion that there is something better out there,... somewhere, is as old as mankind.

A timeless desire to escape domestic ties, seasoned with a mawkish urge to return as the long lost hero is often reflected in great literature, as in "Great Expectations", "Anna Karenina", "Don Quixote". Striving for newness for the sake of newness is one of the cornerstones in the amazing saga of human survival throughout the ages. If we as a race had stayed put and not moved, chances are that we would have been annihilated long time ago. Lack of mobility would have left us much more vulnerable to sudden changes in climate, natural disasters, disease or failing food supplies. Spreading over all the continents made us much more resilient as a race. I will argue that the genetic heritage of restlessness is evolutionarily engrained in us in order to spread the human race over the widest possible area. Looking at our planet today it seems to have worked.

Blame

On my arrival in England to a small, deprived coastal town in the south I met a young man who was as talented as he was lazy. Within minutes of our first meeting he announced with some sympathy that I had arrived to the worst town in Britain. On that cheerful note he continued to explain that this "hole" had been holding him back and it was the reason for why he had not excelled.

The actual place was held responsible for his lack of progress. He aired the notion that if he had been born anywhere else in the whole universe things would have been different. Here he was wrong. Our immediate surroundings are always ready to hand for the blaming of our misfortunes. An objective assessment of the correctness of such an accusation is almost impossible before alternatives have been experienced first hand. If the urge is strong enough, other places will be experienced.

Now, seven years on, the no longer so young man is still living in the same place, uncomfortable at the prospect of losing the best excuse ever invented. Poor him, poor coastal town and poor world that never saw his indisputable talents. Everyone lost.

Casting off the slough
Immigration furthermore offers a truly unique possibility to start afresh at a relatively mature age, with a new world, new people and with no expectations cast in stone. If the role you have played for years seems like a millstone around your neck, like an inescapable baking tin with no room to breath, then changing country and culture may be the answer. No longer are you the hostage of parental or societal expectation. The caveat is as mentioned before: that some people will inadvertently - to variable extents - within a short period of time paint themselves back into the same old corner. That is a long way to go to do that.

In spite of these words of caution it must be emphasised that emigration is a phenomenal chance for shedding an unwanted slough that will not present itself many times over a life span.

Life is good
"Our parents really thought it was a fantastic idea for us to leave for some years… granddad is dying which is why were going back now for a week… he would be very upset if he knew we were interrupting our plans for his sake, so we will just tell him that we had planned to take a break anyway." The words were spoken by two young sisters whom I met on a plane coming back from a skiing holiday. They were

returning to the UK for the sick call after having spent 14 months in the French Alps working, learning French and, not least, skiing. In spite of the difficult circumstances, they both possessed the exuberance of personality that can only flourish with a background of unconditional love, trust and confidence. When questioned on why they had left in the first place they could not come up with a single negative in their 'old world' life worthy of counting for a reason to leave. They felt their Northern Irish coastal town was beautiful, they enjoyed their friends and loved their family, the latter to such an extent that they had chosen to bring a member of the family with them on the journey.

Some immigrants actually break away from their old world not out of spite, not in a specific search for newness or fulfillment of ambitions but simply because old world life is good. It sounds puzzling, but migrating on these happy terms does not make for greater homesickness (see Homesickness). Quite the contrary. Relationships with old world people are for these people often of a strength that can cope with even extended separations if it serves a good purpose. Immigrants of this sort will furthermore expect to walk into loving relationships wherever they go. They are more often right than not.

Stay or go?

The truth of the matter is that we do not know exactly what divides people that take the plunge and emigrate from those who do not. It is also not known if any of the above-mentioned reasons are more important than others in the individual's decision to get up and leave.

Neuro-psychiatric research has shown that people with certain psychiatric conditions are in need of more stimulation than others to maintain focus and a normal state of consciousness. If the individual does not receive enough stimulation in form of changing perceptions, he will do his outmost to create newness. I am not suggesting that emigration is a psychiatric condition, merely that we are probably all placed somewhere on a continuum between craving stimulation and craving security. Only the very severe cases in both directions would be considered pathological. In other words, some people seem to have an inherently lower threshold for boredom and repetition than others, which makes them crave newness in a way that eventually cannot be resisted. It is likely that emigrants belong to this group.

In more provocative terms all these reasons for immigrating can probably be summed up as follows:

For the rich emigrant, as mentioned, the modern 'torment' of absence of suffering becomes so unbearable that something needs to happen, while paradoxically, for the poor immigrant the main reason for emigration remains the presence of suffering.

We need challenges in our lives in order to thrive… and we certainly get that by swapping culture.

Most people leave with their personal combination of all the above mentioned reasons in the bag, usually a mixture of misery and hope. Being mindful of the contents of that bag can turn out to be the best travel insurance you have ever had.

Chapter II

On arrival

"The truth and harmony of the first impression is only permitted once in a lifetime. It has a richness that can and must be shared with others, because beyond the first impression is a sea of knowledge where one can easily drift away and lose sight of all coasts."

Andrei Bitov

Big baby

Arriving in a new country is similar to what it must feel like to be reborn ... in a grown up body. Stripped of your powers to read the cultural signs and clues, often literally speechless and almost entirely dependent on other people's goodwill, you are tearful, easily upset and perhaps even unable to ask for the toilet. It is no longer possible to fabricate a narrative in your mind about the people you meet from their accents, the newspaper they read, they way they dress. The power of gauging other people's character is acutely diminished, which can be very unsettling. It is not unlike being forced to wear a pair of broken glasses; only limited amounts of information will be allowed through and some of that information will be gravely distorted.

Moving the less than 100 km from my home town to Copenhagen to attend university as a young man I initially believed that the majority of the male teachers at the university were gay. Their more sophisticated and animated way of coming across compared to the people with whom I had grown up had me convinced about their sexual orientation in an afternoon. I was entirely wrong. I was misreading signals because I was still wearing my old world glasses. At the time I was unaware that different glasses existed.

More than words

Your new world language is perhaps non-existent or poor. You may get the feeling that the new language is a lethal mixture between Swahili and epilepsy that causes your tongue to swell up to twice its normal size and erases your memory in one clean sweep. And even if you do speak the language, the chances are that you do not understand the local vernacular anyway. The well prepared immigrant has often learned at least some 'new world-ish' either at school or at an adult learning institution – only to discover that the difference between school's 'new world-ish' and the language actual spoken in the country is immense. Even though it may not seem this way initially, learning the basics of a language is, however, never wasted. It will eventually make your progress swifter and your knowledge broader. Furthermore, the natives will always be appreciative of you attempting to speak their language – and thankful for you giving them hours of free amusement.

Disturbed?

Nevertheless, the feeling of being a big, clueless baby, as much in control as a cork screw riding on a tidal wave, can feel humiliating and deeply frustrating and give rise to an unpleasant, but usually groundless sentiment of foreboding. The loss of confidence can be profound. No wonder that some immigrants start to experience rapid mood swings. Previously stable immigrants may suddenly find their mental state oscillating violently between hope and despair. This instability may lead the immigrant to wonder whether a mental illness or a breakdown is underway, which is very rarely the case, especially if there has been no past history of that kind. It helps to systematically go through how many changes you have had to deal with the last period of time. This exercise makes it seem a little less strange that you are a somewhat perturbed.

The ultimate test
It is a testing time. You may at the time feel completely adrift on what seems like a choppy and dangerous ocean with no land in sight. But do not despair. Eleanor Roosevelt believed that nobody could make her feel inferior without her consent. Furthermore, these days, courtesy of modern technology, most oceans have in reality shrunk to garden ponds. A perfectly banal episode such as a rude cashier at the post office or the loss of a wallet can make you burst into tears, and you may start to think that you and your dreams are collapsing all around you. It is frightening how quickly random events at sensitive moments in life can shape our opinions. Opinions which are quickly formed and then solidified by selective information processing.

Accept problems
You have had your normalizing social network removed in one clean sweep. It is no longer possible just to pop round to your best friend and offload to him or her about the silly woman at the post office. All the problems seem to be stranded with you. Lonely problem-solvers have an uncanny tendency of getting things out of proportion. Accept that there are problems, that they are normal in your present situation and do not focus all your energy on them. You will also notice that while in the thick of a difficult situation, say a job interview in a foreign language, an odd surge of "paradoxical confidence" will take hold of you. This is perhaps a mechanism to protect us in extreme situation,

perhaps a mature realization that you are, after all, not as lost as you thought you were.

Remember to do some pleasurable things; meet people, go to the beach, go for a walk in the park. Create a new set of little routines (going to the gym, shopping etc) to console your anxious soul. Remind yourself that your network still exists, albeit not right here. Communicate your distress over the phone, to someone in a similar position to yours or, if necessary, to your neighbour's cat. But clearly, the sooner you manage to build up even a skeleton network of new world people, the sooner will mundane problems again become what they really are, mundane. Know that sometimes you need to be really lost to find yourself.

Higher level

If you manage to struggle through the first difficult time, the price is that your new, extended self will consolidate at a higher level than before you went through the ordeal. You can easily get overwhelmed by the sense of a "life left behind" but do not lose sight of the fact that estrangement can become an immense source of inspiration, inspiration for doggedness, creativity and ultimately self-realization. Someone who goes through a great deal of trouble to obtain something tends to value it more than those who obtain the same thing with less effort. By the way, this "thing" cannot be obtained without going through it. Nietzsche reminds us, that what does not kill us makes us stronger.

Parents will tell you that nothing is more rewarding than watching small kids grow. You have now won the exclusive rights to see yourself go through that process. A few months down the line you will be able to turn around, look into the mirror and say: "Gosh, how I have grown."

Join the new club

The first weeks and months of your stay are crucial to the integration process. The old routines that seemed so dreary and suffocating a few weeks ago, now, in your mind, become the epitome of cosy and safe homeliness. During these trying times being sensitively thick-skinned is an asset. You must find a way to become a member of the new club without having to pay an excessive joining fee. Making yourself available for contact can minimize any early sense of hopelessness. The Danish philosopher Soeren Kierkegaard was adamant that a prerequisite for a fulfilling life was to take a daily "people-bath". This is no less important today than it was when it was written in the early part of the nineteen century.

The isolation you can feel initially in a new country is therefore problem number one to overcome. The lack of social interplay will surprisingly quickly have an influence on your self esteem, which can spiral things into an unnecessary negative circle. The German philosopher Heidegger believed that standing alone was to face the full force of our own mortality. Perhaps belonging to a group is facing the full force of our vitality. Mastering both disciplines will equip you with less fear and more latitude.

Keep your cool

You may feel misunderstood, prejudged and defensive. You may feel people turning away from you either because of language problems or because you are being different. It can leave you irate. It can feel as if there is an acute imbalance between your efforts and the rewards you are harvesting.

If you misunderstand or are misunderstood, keep your cool, do not be embarrassed and ask again. You are, after all, far away from home and cannot be expected to have control of the situation yet.

There will admittedly be moments when you will feel low, lonely and listless. Dig your heels in. Sigmund Freud remarked that we cannot expect to live properly until we know how to die.

After major upheavals in our lives we have a strong tendency to view the world in a relatively negative and defensive way. This can lead to an unconscious calculation that if we do not hope for too much we will be free of disappointment. We are as a race predisposed towards cautious thinking because otherwise we would have been eaten by wild beasts long time ago. This can for a while be a good defence mechanism, but having low expectations can also result in stagnation and lack of progress. Furthermore, this hereditary reticence puts us at risk of bottling out of creating the first contacts. But obtaining contact is a great antidote to negative thinking and even the most modest encounters can be the first important steps in the right direction.

The goal posts have conveniently shifted from the old world life. It is now possible to make contact on the train, in the streets, the parks, sports clubs, bars etc. Your accent will not only serve as a great cover for any kind of embarrassment, it will in addition, provide new acquaintances with a ready-made subject for conservation ("I think I detect a small accent when you speak…"). Once you have realized this new asset you will be difficult to stop.

First day of spring
Even the most trembling immigrant will be titillated by all the bright newness. You cannot help but feel that a new dawn has broken in your life, not unlike the feeling

of euphoria that adds lightness to your step on the first day of spring. However tiny that feeling is, hold on to it with the strength of a bear and the tenderness of a butterfly. Best way of nurturing feelings and ideas is to lift them out of your mind by putting words to them and to discuss them with others. Other immigrants will provide an obvious forum in which to air these thoughts. It is a feeling that can carry you through the darker moments of immigrant life; waiting in the immigration queue, unfriendly individuals, homesickness, sense of insecurity. The settling down period usually takes longer than expected but hopes grown in the honeymoon period and the feeling of empowering newness can be surprisingly difficult to extinguish.

Rarely smoke without a fire

As mentioned earlier, the process of migration has already started long before you left the old world; your parents and other important people in your life may have had certain views about your new country and its people. Just saying the name of some countries, may evoke certain connotations and emotions, usually based on pretty insubstantial, stereotypical hearsay.

Nevertheless, there is rarely smoke without fire, and stereotypes are often built on at least some grain of truth. Many national stereotypes are however often more illustrative of bygone days than they are of the here and now. This is presumably because it takes years for a stereotype to gather impetus and by then, it is already outdated. An excellent example is the disbelief with which English football hooligans are met with during matches abroad. People abroad expect English people to be polite, reserved and to wear bowler hats, even in bed. They do not expect to meet a tattooed skinhead with a beer-belly throwing chairs and tables around. But the hooligans only need to keep up the hard work for another couple of decades before that new stereotype has been cast in stone around the world.

More momentous events like the recent trouble regarding the Danish Muhammad cartoons can change stereotypes overnight. The perception of the Danes as laid-back, Lurpak-producing blondes was dramatically changed in parts of the world by twelve cartoons of Muhammed in an independent Danish newspaper. For many years to come, Danes will be seen in the Arab world as islamophobic blasphemers worthy only of Allah's wrath. According to the demonstrating Muslims, instant beheading seemed to be the preferred method of dealing with the infidels.

Gratuitous madness, some would say. But again, a tiny grain of truth is to be found at the core the pumped-up rhetoric and burning down of Danish embassies. The Danes have not been successful in integrating their minorities, the far right is well represented in the parliament and the level of tolerance is markedly lower than in many other western societies. This provides a dangerous grain of truth that can be exploited by murky characters for their own purposes.

These stereotypes have an influence on the way we prepare ourselves for the journey. The reputation that a nation has back in the old world can undoubtedly either facilitate or hinder later integration. An example of a facilitating reputation could be that South American people are usually seen as friendly and warm people when abroad, while Japanese may generally be viewed as somewhat stern but dedicated workers. I saw a young girl in the streets of London wearing a T-shirt saying: "Kiss me, I am Venezuelan." It is hard to imagine a Japanese giving the same reason for wanting to be kissed.

Stereotypes do not lie down easily. So why not ride on them? Japanese are known to be hard-working. Most stereotypes can, with a little imagination, be swung around in your favour.

Stereotypical attitudes are largely built on hearsay, a few (often distorted) historical facts and, let us not forget, some universally recognized character traits that are typical of that specific culture.

The problem is that stereotypes are one-dimensional and therefore do not by any stretch of the imagination cover the true complexity of the culture we are about to meet - or our own culture that the new world is about to meet.

Be prepared

We run the risk of arriving with a more or less formed image of the new world in our minds that is just waiting to be confirmed. It is therefore recommended that you top up your knowledge about the country to which you are going well before leaving. This can be done by reading travel guides, reading the history of the country, reading books written about new world people, watching films, visiting museums and libraries but most importantly, talking to people who have actually had the experience of living in that culture before. This is especially valuable if these people originate from the same old world as yourself – that will add to the chances of their experience being relevant for you. If time allows, reading literature actually written by authors from the new world culture can add an exclusive insight into the people with whom you will soon be living.

Bringing a few photos of your family and friends, the house you were living in and important places in your country will be illuminating for people you meet in the new world. This has nothing do with boring people to tears with three volumes of the family photo albums – just a little taster of where you are from. A photo of you aged three always goes down well.

It works both ways
Just as you have had ideas about them, the new world inhabitants will have preconceived ideas about you simply because of the country from which you come. Their views are usually stereotyped but may also be coloured by personal experiences. These views can be difficult to escape from but, as mentioned, can almost always be turned in your favor.

In the mid-nineties, while planning a stay in Paris I was amazed to find that the clinical director of the big hospital to which I was applying was unwilling to accept me on the simple grounds that I was Danish.

Being a man schooled before the era of political correctness he said, to my astonishment, exactly that. When I inquired into why this was the case he told that he had had two Danish doctors on his staff in the past and they had both been disastrous.

That was at least straight talking. The sense of brain-dead injustice had nevertheless infuriated me to such a degree that I immediately grabbed the phone and called another powerful man in the hospital. I explained my situation to him and got the job without further delay – more because the other powerful man was embarrassed on his colleague's behalf than because of my credentials.

Ironically, after an initial period of mutual suspicion, the American and I became very good friends after he realized that I was not just what he considered to be "Danish". All credit to his willingness to reassess.

General values

Reluctantly, I have to admit that the old, distinguished, American doctor had a point… up to a point. Within the same culture we do all tend to develop a relatively similar way of processing many fundamental situations, e.g. how we view what is acceptable behaviour, how we obtain friends and partners and simply what we assess to be important in life: in other words, general values. However, within every culture, in this case a nation-culture, there are numerous sub-cultures that my American boss so conveniently overlooked; clearly the Danish branch of Hells Angels shares only few values with members of the Danish Needlework Association. In fact, you could argue that every individual represents a distinct culture in himself and perhaps even different cultures depending on the situation.

My American boss failed to grasp these subtleties in spite having lived abroad for over 30 years himself. I nevertheless felt a strong desire to prove him wrong. My spotless work record during my Paris time seemed a vindication not only for me as an individual, but also on behalf of my nation which honour had been soiled.

Maybe the old American was more cunning than I thought at first. By insulting my national pride he had me working ten times as hard for the same money. No threats, no disciplinary hearings were necessary, just a few initial, obnoxious comments and he had me working like a madmen in the name of my fatherland. Clever clogs.

Age

Biological age is often cited as a defining factor for how successful the integration process will be. It is a truth with modifications. Clearly, things are going to be more difficult if you health is poor and getting around is problematic. I have seen many well-integrated pensioners who left their old world only relatively recently. A common feature of these late immigrants is a determination to learn the language, a balanced love of their new culture and some degree of fearlessness. A common feature for unsuccessful late – and younger – immigrants, is not having done their homework (what will I miss, what can be gained), an uncritical admiration for the new world ("the sun always shines out there") combined with ill-considered unwillingness to or fear of learning new things.

Children pay the price

Children are commonly the hapless pawns in their parents' wish for a new life. A Portuguese friend told me that when she arrived in France at the age of three she was sent to kindergarten where all she remembered was laughing because she found all the French kids very stupid. They did not understand Portuguese. But generally speaking, it is, unfortunately, a widespread myth that kids will just play in the schoolyard for a few weeks and then speak the language fluently. Not so – at least not for the slightly older children. Children are rarely "motivated" to uproot in the way grown-ups are; they do think there is much reason to leave their little friends in the street, the school the like, the language with which they have just become confident. They may not see the bigger picture and it is not their fault.

The benefits in the longer term can be immense for the younger generation. Bilingual children do better in verbal and non-verbal tests, have greater meta-linguistic awareness and cognitive flexibility. Bilingualism improves memory and may even protect against Alzheimer's. In all the excitement about all the benefits the emotional and psychological toll on the child can so easily be overlooked. But make no mistake about it, bringing children along to the new world can be so painful for everyone that the whole project can come to grief on this one issue. '

Some Dutch friends had three kids of which the eldest was a daughter. Over the three years she lived here she seemed to change from being a beautiful, confident little girl to a frightened, tearful, nervous wreck. She fell behind at school, never obtained a comfortable level of English and was too timid to make friends. To her, the English experience was an all-out assault on her sense of self-esteem and security.

The two younger boys in the family seemed to take much the same approach as the Portuguese girl above. Their integration appeared to run as smoothly as their sister's did not. In the end the parents decided that enough was enough and the whole family returned to the Netherlands, even though the father's career would have been greatly enhanced by staying. Having visited the family, happily settled in a peaceful village in their old world, it seems the girl is back to her old self – perhaps still with a persistent hint of anxiety that seems out of character with the rest of the family.

Tell it to them straight
Careful preparation for the journey is essential, even for tiny children. They should be told very openly that this is not going to be easy for a very long while. They should also be told about the possible benefits to their lives and that of their parents. Passing on the excitement felt by the grown up for the move is a skill – passing on anxieties is innate. Keeping the connections to the old world open – inviting little friends to come and stay and vice versa - is critical. It takes an effort, but keeping your child on side can make all the difference.

Overcoming the challenges of integration is probably done with more easily when you are young but older people have life experience that can serve them well. Local knowledge obtained in your distant home town can be put to good use during late life integration. Integration has no optimal age – just an optimal attitude.

Stereotyping

Stereotyping is a vice that in our present, stifling climate of political correctness is harshly condemned. Categorizing fellow human beings into certain boxes is wrong, we are told. *That* is wrong. Stereotyping is an innate feature of human perception that has been with a person from a very early age; this is simply the way young children learn to use their memory by storing different item under certain "headings", e.g. red, blue, green under colours, cat, dog, cow under animals etc. In other words, an immensely useful filing system that over time in evolution has been reinforced by its user-friendliness.

To expect that with a single stroke of official, political correctness we can eradicate that way of thinking is naïve. However, a reasonable expectation is that the above-mentioned filing system becomes a little more sophisticated in the grown-up. Information about diversity, equal rights and the advantages of cooperation must be given at an early stage in life.

A projection

The last years have in the western world seen an uncompromising policy of zero acceptance of stereotyping. The predictable outcome has been that the practice of stereotyping has gone underground in the educated classes, while the lower classes generally are finding it more difficult to hide. People in charge will quite happily deny treating people from different backgrounds differently, even though few believe them. The political correctness does however rarely reach its prime target; the more vulnerable groups in the host countries are usually confronted more with poorer emigrants than are the ruling classes who preach liberal tolerance. These groups therefore often deliver the most vociferous outbursts against immigrants, sometimes using offensive stereotypes. Because the host country's underdog group feels threatened they will start projecting ills onto the new group of people that so conveniently have turned up on the shores to take the blame for different ills in society. But the accuser is seldom innocent.

Deadly weapon
Stereotyping is a big seller. The media loves it. Over recent years lives have been lost as a result of hateful stereotyping spurred on by a media-frenzy against, for example, asylum seekers, who have been tried and convicted by the mob. Stereotyping may be a natural part of human nature but in the wrong hands it can be turned into a deadly weapon.

The political correctness that seeks to sweep differences between cultures under the carpet is a romantic fallacy, no better than the nineteenth century notion of the "noble savage". It seems clear that such an approach did not lead to greater equality or happiness for anyone involved. The same is the case today. Open acknowledgement of differences is a much more sincere and healthy approach than eternal denial.

Ignorance
Stereotyping takes place at different levels and sometimes appears indistinguishable from ignorance. A

happy acquaintance of mine storms up to me and proudly announces that he is just back from Amsterdam! "Wonderful city".

"Great for you, mate, but I am not from Holland", I responded.

"But I thought you said you were Dutch... or did you say Danish, isn't that the same?"

In the presence of a late family member I complimented an Asian looking news reader on Danish television for pronouncing a difficult Arab place name. "Well," he said, "that isn't so strange, she is also from down there."

Yes, but perhaps not necessarily from the "same down there". In the old man's mind there were us and them – them being everyone that was not Danish. This kind of stereotyping is the product of ignorance and indifference. Not only ignorance but also indifference can be helped by gentle education. And made worse by pontification.

The bigger picture

The international hierarchy mentioned previously has a more or less global flavor. It is however useful to take stock of the national variations on the theme of stereotyping other countries. Making fun of your immediate neighbours is an international sport that almost all countries take very seriously. The rules are simple and the victim largely absent. The aim is for the home nation to come out on top. It is an amazingly popular game even for people of normal intelligence. In my native Denmark we make fun of the Swedes, though they in turn quite like us. The Danes suffer from a notorious "little-brother'' syndrome that will not be put to rest despite several recent victories in football over their "arch-rivals". According to the myth, the Swedes are supposed to be tedious, alcoholic and humourless. You will actually hear well-educated Danes put forward such views at otherwise respectable dinner parties. The truth is that it reflects more of a sense of inferiority rather than actual disdain. This phenomenon is known from other neighbouring countries of differing powers, New Zealand-Australia, Canada-USA.

Learn the rules
It is helpful to achieve an idea about the popular conceptions of other countries in your new world country at an early stage during the integration process. The relationship between England and Ireland took me quite by surprise when I first arrived in the UK. Admittedly the basis of the problems between these two nations is at least partly based on relatively recent, historical facts. The ferocity of the jokes leaves the neutral observer in no doubt about the depth of the animosity. Jokes about the Irish are treated with the same seriousness as any other racist remarks both by the BBC and the police, a fact that of course only adds to their attraction. While it would be ill-advised for the immigrant to play along with these preconceptions, making a mental note of them will allow you to grasp yet another part of your new world, national character.

I am still to this day on occasions confronted with "Hoediboehdi" when people hear my accent. It is supposed to be a joke which alludes to the Swedish cook in the Muppet Show. Often the new world people I come across are blissfully unaware that Swedish is not the same as Danish, and equally unaware that Swedish, when well spoken, is one of the most melodic and beautiful languages in the world. My reaction is usually one of a strained smile followed by an often fruitless attempt to put them right. One of my current neighbors continues to harass me with this infamous

"Hoediboehdi-Hoediboehdi". He will shout it over the fence, hum it while he is walking by my house and even knock on my windows and sing away in an aborted attempt to sound Swedish. He is incorrigible. Any educational approach seems lost on him. Frederick the Great believed that if you drove out prejudices by the door, they would return by the window. James quite literally does. James is 5 years old.

Education is the medicine
A more subversive level of stereotyping is also built on ignorance, but used on a political scale. Foreign people can be portrayed as useless parasites and all tarred with the same brush regardless of different background. This is just downright stupidity that threatens not only the newcomers but also the country the xenophobics pretend to protect. Loss of integration results in loss of productive activity. Again, education is the preferred medicine, this time combined with public vigilance towards persecution.

It can be exasperating to be talked about as the "bloody foreigner". During a stint as a tennis coach in the French Alps I heard my boss talking to someone about "le danois" (the Danish), one of the few French words I understood at the time. I also heard, and understood, the word "merde" (shit). I gathered that those two words in close proximity was not a good sign at all. I had failed to be seen by him as anything else than a shitty Dane that misunderstood his instructions. Had I been able to humanise myself by passing on my personal story more effectively I believe the situation would have been different. Breaking away from the anonymous sea of foreigners descending on the new world country is to a large degree your own responsibility. It takes language, individuality and tenacity. You are ripping off the mask of anonymity handed out by the immigration process. By the way, the French tennis pro did not sack me … before the following week.

Nothing new under the sun
Every society has some early reticence about accepting newcomers. Admittedly, the difficulties penetrating the preliminary walls of suspicion can differ wildly from culture to culture, and the process can take from days to decades, to death. It is not unlike an initiation ceremony in a fraternity that initially harasses would-be brothers. If you can cope with it, it will eventually heighten your commitment to the group which is probably the unconscious aim of initially stand-offish behaviour. Your main objectives are very basic: show them friendliness and that you have something to offer the community. My fellow country man, the comedian Victor Borge, used to say, that the shortest distance between people is a smile.

It is not unusual for perfectly innocent people to have to take the responsibility of a whole nation on their shoulders in the new world. Often this is the good-humored context of a sports competition or the like. It can however also take the form of ignorant, malicious remarks about distant historical or even current political events on which the poor immigrant has no influence.

A young Italian friend of mine recently arrived in England was harangued by some other tennis playing friends because of the latest gaffes of his old world Prime Minister.

"How can you elect a Prime Minister like that?"

"Well, I did not vote for…"

"Yeah, but I mean it is disgusting what he says about the Jews. Are you all like that down there?"

"I don't agree with that."

"What? You don't agree with me?

"No, no, I…"

"Hi, listen, mate that guy is just downright crazy, he runs the country as if he's the head of the bloody mafia."

Clearly ill-at-ease with the discussion that was rather one-sided due to the Englishman's perseverance and the Italian's poor English skills, my Latin friend left the club house keen to get back on court where the language is more international. He served a lot of aces that day.

Sense of weakness

The example shows how a minority of new world people detects a sense of weakness – here language skills – and jumps on the chance of finally being in a position of power. One often gets the sense that a poor immigrant's language problems presents to this group of new world people a rare opportunity to feel they are firmly in the driving seat. The advantage is exploited to an extent that paradoxically leaves the exploiter more disadvantaged than the exploited.

There is a fine balance to be struck between recognizing a national character and stereotyping.

Ambassador

Whether you like it or not, you will be regarded as an ambassador for your country. It is said that a good ambassador is an honest man that lies for his country. That kind of approach cannot be recommended; it is sufficient to be an honest man who stands up for his country. You may be the first person from that country with whom the new world people have come into contact. People will automatically associate you and your behaviour with your nationality. They will most probably, 20 years down the line when they meet another person from your country say: "Oh, yeah, I use to know a person from x-land… he was always blah-blah." What the blah-blah is, is up to you.

Sometimes the heavy responsibility is welcomed by the newly appointed "ambassador". A short time ago I was checking out of a hotel in London and I asked the young girl in the reception where she was from. "Germany" was the shy answer and she hastily added: "But I am not typically German," suggesting that she was all too well aware of the social stereotypes that especially in the past was associated with being German. An over-emphasis on stereotypes predisposes heavily to two of the migrant's death sins, copying of the new world or over-pride in your old world. Often in an ugly blend that does nothing for the countries or for you.

The human mind
The human mind is by definition lazy and therefore much prefers being confirmed in its hypothesis than having to construct a new one! Having to rethink the whole situation takes a lot of energy. The more entrenched a certain way of thinking has become the more difficult it will be to change. In addition, there is undoubtedly a peculiar thrill associated with confirmation of a dearly-held hypothesis. Therefore it does take an extra effort to step out of the heavy armour of expectation - both theirs and yours – and experience things your way. Even though that negative stereotyping is more important to get to grips with, sometimes our positive preconceptions can be as detrimental as they can lead to some serious disappointments. To deal with the challenges of arrival I have, in chapter three, lined up some key points on how to - and how *not* to - deal with the new world upon arrival.

Chapter III

Dos and don'ts.

*"When house and land are gone and spent,
then learning is most excellent."*
English 18th century proverb

Guidance

It may seem as an extraordinary act of arrogance to line up a list of ways on how to behave and not to behave during the early stages of immigration. So it is. But there are undoubtedly certain skills that can be further developed or acquired in order to make the initial period more enjoyable and rewarding.

I am by no means claiming that the list is exhaustive or without mistakes but there clearly are certain behaviours that can both advance or obstruct our lives. In spite of cultural differences, these behaviours are relatively global and serve as oil on the social wheel. It goes however without saying that the welcome cries of some societies are louder than others and that the skills mentioned can always benefit from improvisation and different doses of local flavor.

Behaviour is to a large extent shaped by personal experiences. But at no point is it more important to be receptive than when you first arrive in a new country. Behaviour is hence a question of trial and error, a bit like trying on different clothes to see how they please you and others. There is no reason not to learn from others' experiences and then attach your own personal slant. I believe that the advice listed below can hurry you along towards a more satisfying level of integration.

Don't be arrogant

Not to be confused with being self-confident (see dos). Arrogance is to believe that one is superior combined with a willingness to convey that impression in contact with others. It is traditionally interpreted as the way the insecure handles life. It is undoubtedly true that people who for some reason or another feel under pressure can choose to appear arrogant as a coping mechanism. A very bad coping mechanism. Putting on an armour of "protective arrogance" comes more natural to some than others when under pressure. To keep the looming sense of incompetence at arm's length, an often subconscious, selective focus on all the strong sides of one's personality can be adopted. If you have been criticised for this in the past, it is extra relevant to be on the look out for apparent signs of arrogance reoccurring during emigration.

In my experience, arrogance can actually also be born out a genuine belief in a person's own superiority - more or less rooted in reality. The arrogant person will mistakenly believe that his superior competence in one area (e.g. knowledge of literature, ability to run fast, good looks) has, for no good reason at all, suddenly generalised into all other aspects of life.

Whatever its origin, arrogance has a stifling influence on human relationships. As a newcomer in a society it is recommended that you be on guard for any signs of arrogance in your own behaviour - especially self-acclamatory stories about previous conquests. Not only do they bore others to tears, but the first impression may have a negative long term impact on your relationships in the new world.

The locals in even the most accommodating society will always be vigilant towards arrogance in strangers, perhaps with an underlying attitude of "Don't come and tell us what to do in our own country". If arrogance is found, the consequences can be rather severe; a bad reputation, a hostile or cool atmosphere when encountering the natives. You will soon learn that different societies have different levels of acceptance of arrogance but before you have a good grasp of the local level, a wait-and-see policy is advisable. This is really a key part of painless integration. Rather underplay your game for a little longer than risking your reputation with a few, early off-the-cuff remarks.

Don't be frustrated with your own frustration
It may feel overpowering, and indeed disempowering, having to adapt to all the new impressions, new language, new customs, loss of status, different set of values and so on. It is always tempting to allow the frustration to take over and let it guide you straight into the nearest travel agency to buy a return ticket. But it is perhaps the very most crucial part of integration to be able to live with and contain frustration.

It is, paradoxically, exactly the anger and sense of hopelessness that in the longer perspective will make you pull through. Frustration can be an important source of energy in situations where you feel you have had enough of everything. Grit your teeth and promise yourself that "This will not get the better of me".

It is useful to make a parallel to our ancient past; creativity is at its peak in situations of need. Creativity would be an absolute necessity if you were caught on an island full of dangerous predators and the only way out was to get across to the mainland. You would be pushed into finding something that could float, sail or somehow carry you across, maybe in co-operation with other people in a similar position. Likewise in the immigrant's situation. You are pushed to the limit, and beyond, but you will find strength and ingenuity that you did not know you had. And that feels good.

It has often been discussed why such a large proportion of the world's great art seem to arise from people in some kind of emotional pain. It is highly likely that some of the same processes are in play here. Small grains of sand can by the oyster be turned into beautiful pearls.

Large population surveys have repeatedly revealed that immigrants do better socially than the indigenous, new world people in spite of the immigrants' humble backgrounds, both financially and educationally. The frustration and possible perception of humiliation have driven these people forward – they have a point to prove. The history books are full of examples of successful immigrants from all over the world; the Huguenots around Europe, the Jews all over the world, the Asians in Africa. Common to all these people is that they proudly brought their own culture with them – without letting it overshadow the integration process. Their superior performance seemed to be linked to an understanding that becoming socially competent in a new culture does not mean losing the same competence in the culture of origin, quite the contrary.

By going abroad you do create a kind of artificial survival exercise that will challenge your adaptability and – if you have the guts – will change your life forever. Necessity is truly the mother of all invention - and creativity.

Don't play the race/xenophobia card
- unless it is absolutely necessary!

I recently placed an advert in automobile magazine in the hope of selling my old car. To my horror I realized the editors had written that the car had done

77000 miles instead of the correct 7700 miles. I had placed the advertisement over the phone and I immediately started to question myself about whether it was my accent that had let me down. The tension was building over the weekend during which I was unable to contact the magazine office. The car had to be sold before I went on holiday the following week. On the Monday morning I called the woman in the office that I originally had spoken to and explained my situation. The woman readily accepted responsibility and said that she could not understand how that had happened. Out of sheer anxiety I asked her if my accent had been the reason for the misunderstanding. Her friendly small talk stopped abruptly, and I could hear her pause to consider what the right response would be. I had unconsciously played the xenophobia card and it had hit the poor woman right between her eyes. In this country, like in many other western societies, a strong wind of political correctness is blowing across the nation. Woe to anyone that tries to step out of line. Finally, she answered in an aloof and terse voice that the mistake would be corrected for the following week's edition and she apologized for the mistake in a way that could not have been more robotic if she had tried.

I hung up with an unpleasant feeling of having done something wrong – used a sledgehammer to crack a nut (or as we say in Danish: "shoot a sparrow with a canon"). I was concerned that I had scared the woman who was by now probably fearing for her job.

Being racist/xenophobic is not taken lightly in the UK these days. A single call to her boss could have put her in trouble. As I considered calling her up or writing a letter to explain that I did not mean it so seriously, I received the following week's car magazine: "Vauxhall Corsa, 2002, only 77000 miles…"

People feel bullied by the threat of being blamed for something. Bullying rarely leads to an increase in efficiency, which my dealings with the lady at the car magazine so poignantly illustrated. Playing the race card usually leads to increased suspicion and artificial niceties. You usually get your way the first time it is done, but people will not feel comfortable in your company again. An artificial, politically correct ambience is created in which people feel policed and un-free. Policing only adds to the complainer's alienation. You will be regarded as the little boy who grasses up on his friends to the teacher on playground duty. Of course there are extreme situations that need official intervention from above, but as a rule of thumb, stop being a victim. It will not help you, it will not move society forward. It is better to deal with possible, discriminatory situations on your own accord with a mixture of humour, dignity and – every once in a while - biting your tongue. Choose your conflicts with care.

Absurdly enough, discrimination is not confined to living abroad. Anti-foreign feelings have for a long time been rife in many countries in Europe. A little example drawn from my own experiences as junior doctor in a Copenhagen hospital illustrates this perfectly. At 4am after a gruelling on-call on the medical ward I was called to the admission ward to take a blood-gas test on an elderly lady with chronic asthma. A blood-gas test needs to be taken from an artery which is quite a lot more complicated and painful for the patient than an ordinary blood test taken in a superficial vein. On top of this, I was inexperienced and exhausted. All of this led to approximately ten failed attempts for the poor woman whose breathing was not helped by the young Dr Hansen's inaptitude. Out of the corner of my eyes I realized that we were not alone in the room. A large, elderly man suddenly rose from a chair to his feet in a dimly light corner of the room and said: "Hold it right there, Dr Hassan... I have now been paying tax to the Danish state for the last forty years and I demand to see a Danish doctor, *NOW* ... and as far as you are concerned you can take the next train back to Istanbul where you bloody came from".

Dr Hassan/Hansen did not feel like arguing and went to get his senior on call who sorted out the problem straight away without any further ado. My senior on call that night was a hefty, 6'6" tall Nigerian doctor with whom all derogatory and racist comments would have been ill placed.

Don't be paranoid
Or at least not more paranoid than necessary! I realize that that is easier said than done because in many ways it's a very natural position; if animals are removed from their original habitat to a new place they will invariably enter an endemic state of hypervigilance, constantly on the look out for possible dangers. Anything else would be foolish. Complacency could soon land them in a predator's belly.

These evolutionary traits are still with us today. Paranoia comes from Greek and literally means being "beside one's mind". In our modern day understanding of the word it means the fear that someone – usually for no good reason at all – is out to harm you or your loved ones. We become unduly self-referential and misperceive irrelevancies as threatening signals.

Since the time of mass immigration to the USA in the early 20th century it has been known that immigrants are more at risk of developing paranoid states needing medical intervention than people who stay put in their native country. This fact has been further corroborated by high-quality research into Afro-

Caribbean immigration into the United Kingdom in the latter part of the 20th century.

There are essentially three possible explanations. Either the immigrants are under excessive pressure; not speaking the local language, detached from their culture and loved ones, and perhaps even looking different. Or, there is an overrepresentation amongst immigrants of people with difficult personalities and with a predisposition to develop mental problems. In other words, people who do not fit in easily into society, even their own, are more likely to emigrate in the first place. A combination of the two causes is probably present in most cases of serious immigration-paranoia.

The third option is that the immigrant actually has real reason to be suspicious - as the poor Austrian queen of France, Marie Antoinette so horribly discovered in the frantic days of the French revolution in the 1790s. Married to Louis 16th at the tender age of 15, the French never forgave her for being foreign. She was believed to be conspiring with her Austrian compatriots against the state of France, even though that the reality was that she had no political interest at all.

After a short, initial period of adoration she fell out of favour with the French people who regarded her as a debauchee, frivolous and prodigal. Whether this description bears any resemblance to the real Marie Antoinette is still today hotly debated by historians. What is beyond discussion is that she served as an excellent scapegoat for all the ills of a hopelessly backward, feudal system that by the end of the 18th century had left the majority of French people living in desperate poverty. Here was this foreign woman literally in bed with the father of the nation, begging to be targeted as the cause of most problems, the enemy within who conveniently could be pointed out in the crowd because of her differentness. Interestingly, the killings did not stop with the decapitation of Marie Antoinette. The revolutionaries had by killing her lost a valuable scapegoat and swiftly needed new ones.

The corollary of the story is that we can be easy targets as foreigners for malevolent rumors, and therefore not all paranoia felt by immigrants is entirely unfounded. It is as unpleasant as it is unsettling, but once again represents a great opportunity for quick learning. Certain scenarios exist where the emigrant is simply a pawn in a bigger game out of the individual's control. But there are clearly situations where steering clear of unwarranted targeting can be achieved by using your best social and diplomatic skills combined with a good sense of when not to care.

Don't jump to conclusions

You could be walking down the street and suddenly feel "unduly self-referential". You get the unpleasant feeling that the man in the barber's shop is staring at you for longer than you like. You try to not look but cannot help turning your head to see if your hunch is right. Bang, eye contact.

Your heart starts beating a bit faster. You take a few more steps, and this time you turn all the way round in order to confront him. Yes, he is still staring at you and he is even bloody laughing. How dare he! You take a deep breath and step forward to have a word with cheeky bugger.

STOP! Please, think before you act. Maybe he *was* looking at you! But who is to say what he was thinking? He may not have been looking at you for the hostile reasons that can be imagined in the mind of a scared newcomer. For all you know, he may have a visual impairment, he may be thinking about something completely different, he may not have been laughing but attempting to smile to emphasise his friendly intentions. He may have noticed that you are looking at him or he may even been thinking that you are a sexy thing and that he wants to give you his phone number.

Another common situation is when you feel that people at work are getting fed up with your poor language skills. You feel that they are condescending towards you and suspect that they may be talking about you and your pathetic, new world language behind your back. At work they only give you menial tasks because they think you are thick. This is how it appears to you. In psychological terms it is called appraisal bias, which plainly means that you are getting the wrong end of the stick.

Forcing yourself to look at the situation from different angles is therapeutic. Could it be that your work colleagues are trying to speak slowly and clearly to make sure you understand? That they are talking about how best to help you "behind your back" and that they give you do-able jobs in order not scare you off? The focus on your inadequacies may be yours, not theirs.

It is therefore absolutely essential to allow yourself to contemplate alternative explanations as to why new world people treat you the way that they do. In the early period of our time abroad we are clearly more prone to jump to unsubstantiated conclusions about our new fellow country men because of our own insecurities and our sense of standing out.

The French author Annis Ninn said, that things are not the way they are, they are the way *we* are. In other words, our paranoia is often a reflection of inner turmoil due to having left everything we knew and been thrown in at the deep end of a pond you do not know.

The best remedy for paranoid tendencies and hasty conclusions is again contact with the alleged perpetrators, new world people. It is amazing how fast trust can be restored through a hearty laugh across language and culture barriers.

This paragraph will be rounded off with one of my own hard-earned experiences on foreign ground. As a tired junior doctor in a Parisian hospital I was having a late dinner in the canteen after a maddeningly busy day. Four or five workmen that I had never seen before were sitting a couple of tables away laughing and joking with each other. I did not pay much attention to them until one of them lit up a cigarette.

The restaurant was covered in signs saying "Defense de fumer" (Smoking prohibited). As the avid anti-smoker I am, I shouted across the tables that he should put out his "coffin nail" immediately. The smoking man waved at me and took a long draw of his cigarette and blew the smoke slowly out in my direction. The men appeared to be laughing at my expense.

I was absolutely enraged at this stage. I attempted to continue my meal, but the anger soon got the better of me. I hammered the cutlery down onto my plate, got up and walk briskly towards the men with the intention of not only putting the cigarette out, but putting it somewhere where cigarettes are not intended to go!

As I got to their table in all my youthful might, hands on hips, I started to shout at the top of my voice about what I thought of their behaviour and what I would like to do with the still burning cigarette. The men had by now stopped their conversation and looked anxiously at me. Not anxious about what my plans for them were, but anxious about my mental health. Their facial expressions of timid helpfulness infuriated me even further, and I was just about pull up my sleeves and become violent when the smoking man in a quietly inquisitive voice in broken French said: "I no speaking French."

I felt rather deflated as I returned to my table having cowardly abandoned giving any explanations for my bombastic behavior. The men who were of Arab decent had not understood a single word of my wild ranting and raving - just as they had not understood the non-smoking signs on the wall. They were clearly recent immigrants to France from some Arab nation. The smoking man had however hastily put out his cigarette and continued to look in my direction with a mixture of disbelief and compassion. Without being the slightest bit paranoid I am to this day convinced that the men thought I was an escaped maniac from a local secure institution. My appetite had deserted me and soon after I left the restaurant with a shuffling gait.

This little episode had done nothing to further my integration into French society and I presume, the Arab men's neither - especially not if they thought I was French.

The feeling of paranoia spans the whole spectrum from a vague sense of apprehension to severe agitation and fear. For the vast majority of new-comers the creepy feeling of paranoia stays at a manageable level and only a minority has not experienced some degree of it during the first period of time away in a new culture. It leads to the kind of hyper-vigilance that is tiring but far from pathological. The usual course is a slow decline of the concern over time, with fluctuations related to specific events. But eventually, more energy will be freed up to do other things.

Don't disappear without a trace
At no stage in your life than when you migrate is it truer that you *are* the link between your past and your

future. It is a responsibility that should be taken seriously. The interconnectedness between the different stages in your life must be nurtured like a frail flower that without attention would wither away. This is especially important for people who leave with an excess baggage of hate and anger. Modern technology eases considerably the practical problems of keeping in touch, while the emotional problems sometimes take some swallowing.

Neglecting your past will reduce not only your memories but also you as a person. Maintaining contact will give you a sense of the distance you covered as well as keeping relationships alive. The effort that it takes to keep in contact with selected people in your old world will add to your new world experiences and to the person the new world will meet. Watering flowers that you planted a long time ago will make you more whole. Withering flowers are a sad and unnecessary sight.

Do be genial and frank
Open friendliness is probably the most essential of all ingredients in all human contact. It may be the last thing you want to be if you feel threatened and worried about the whole situation just after arriving. But it is an endeavour that is well worth your while, and when started it becomes self-perpetuating. Being approachable has to do with eye contact, gestures and smiles. You do not necessarily have to be overly polite and correct all the time. Doing and saying things that are not in the script take a certain expertise but will leave your personal signature in people's mind. Even without great language skills you can still make an effort to appear ready to engage with the new world people. Approachability makes people attractive.

The differences between you and them can seem so overpowering, especially initially. Build a bridge. Showing warm interest in their lives is always a winner, seen from both perspectives. People love to talk about their lives, attitudes and aspirations, while you learn about new world life and the optimal way of communicating with new world people.

Do enter into debates about differences between the new and the old world, but keep in mind that the aim of a debate is not victory but mutual progress. It can be a very effective learning experience to discuss your perception in a frank manner with an equally frank person from either the new or the old world.

Even though courteousness is recommended at all times it is certainly not a good idea to behave in a submissive and spineless manner.

When the situation calls for it you should be prepared to explain to your new world friends in a non-dogmatic way about the origin of your differentness and why you feel the way that you do. It does however have to be finely balanced every time in order to avoid unnecessary conflict. Discussions about elusive, national character traits always carry the risk of becoming more emotional than rational. The fear of heated confrontation should not prevent us from discussing these issues in a civilized manner, as there is far more to lose from abstaining. A tragic example of the loss that can be incurred is when immigrants are unwilling to bring any of their own cultural heritage with them to the new world. The reason for this self-eradication is commonly some inner experience of inferiority – not necessarily concerning the person's own confidence but rather how his society of origin is viewed in the new world. This judgment of value of a society is, as mentioned, often made on its economic strength, state of development and to some extent cultural output and history. Measures of these quantities are not easily measurable, but people have an uncanny sixth sense with regard to picking up on their own position in any pecking order.

It is wise though to use the adjectives as "better" and "worse" with the outmost care in open discussion and reserve them for use with closer friends. And even here caution should prevail, otherwise close friends may very soon become ex-friends. The shrewd settler quickly learns how to operate in these troubled waters to everyone's benefit.

Do get a grip on the local etiquette…

… without changing your basic values in the process. I was recently invited out to an Indian colleague's house where I met his two adorable daughters aged 9 and 11. The whole family had not long ago arrived to England for the parents to work. The girls were very confident and keen to show me how life is lived, songs are song and food is eaten in India. After the meal that we ate with the fingers, the older of the girls wanted to show "uncle", as they called me, an Indian dance. The little sister took her place on my lap loudly applauding the dancing sister. This was not all she was doing loudly. The little beauty was belching and farting away at a pace and volume that would have left any 20 stone rugby player seriously envious. Nobody could have predicted that a tiny body like hers harboured such an awe-inspiring display of fireworks. It was not easy to keep my composure but nevertheless important for the other girl not to believe that I was laughing at her dancing.

Clearly, before she hits her teenage years, this girl will grasp that Europeans are still very prudish and embarrassed about their bodily functions. She will learn this for her own sake, rather than for that of others. It is likewise important that we as immigrants should, as soon as possible, get some idea about the local customs in the new world. Engaging as much as possible with new world people will give you the chance to pick up the tricks and refine your own approach both culturally and linguistically. But do not despair if you go wrong every now and again, take it with a smile and learn your lesson. Relearning as a grown-up takes persistence.

Walking home from the visit to my Indian friends I personally took the girl's outlets with more than a smile, actually I laughed so heartedly that by-passers started to stare.

Do learn the new language…

… as soon and as well as possible. *No* viable excuse for not doing so exists. Not speaking the language can make you feel terribly trapped and desperate – your thoughts and emotions unable to cross the barbed wire of the language barrier. You feel restricted and that your wings have been clipped. You can no longer push the buttons that were second nature to you back in the old world. Other buttons fortunately exist.

The language is the key that will open doors for you both socially and professionally. No culture can be conquered without the necessary language skills. Most countries have organized language courses of varying quality. Check out a particular course's credentials – preferably by talking to previous students - before signing up. A language course can also be an excellent way of meeting other people in a similar situation to you. The drawback is the temptation to talk with fellow students in your own language or in any other mutual second language not relevant to the new world. This is a common trap that should be avoided at all costs.

You can always ask people in the new world for advice. I am yet to meet a single person that got annoyed when asked for advice on pronunciation or semantics. It actually makes local people quite proud that they can help. Furthermore, it sends out a clear signal of your eagerness to learn and integrate. Like house-proud owners showing friends around their home for the first time, they will show you the ins and outs of their linguistic quarters, where to tread carefully, where to relax and where to cook up a bigger meal.

Even in a world of modern technology a minimum of two dictionaries, new world language – old world language *and* the other way around is a must. It would also be advisable to own a comprehensive dictionary of the new world language on its own too.

Every time you come across a word or an expression you do not know – or are not sure of - look it up. The same advice relates to old world expressions that may appear in your head while you are attempting to express something in new world language. Do not just take the easy way out and find some way around the missing expression. Look it up or ask people around. It can be quite painstaking at first, but little by little you will experience how your investment pays off; you come across expressions a second time while reading or talking that you previously have looked up and it gives an immediate rush of satisfaction and a sense of progress. Depending on your initial level of knowledge of the language you will over a period of time start to feel that you can actually communicate with these people. It is a truly remarkable sensation that is not surpassed by many other emotions in the human repertoire.

Grammar is the thorny subject that most people vaguely recall from school with a mixture of trepidation and embarrassment. Using some time on understanding the building stones of the language is time well spent. Things will suddenly fall into place and make a lot more sense. The principles of grammar are pretty universal and can be transferred to the next language you want to learn.

Do keep talking

Your reading speed never really seems to reach the same level as in old world-ish. It will take longer to get through the syllabus than it would have done back home. Students beware.

Some years ago while I was working in old-age psychiatry, an old Polish man spent months on the ward waiting for a rest home place. I had become quite friendly with his extended family and especially with his gorgeous four-year old grandson who was often bored during the long visits to the ward. With the dual intention of entertaining and educating the little boy about his Polish heritage, his grandparents had given him a video of what seemed to be a Polish children's film from the 1950s. Passing the television lounge, the boy grabbed hold of me and demanded that I sit down and read the English subtitles aloud to him as he did not speak a word of his grandparents' language. I happily obliged, to dodge the more menial task of the working day. But the boy soon despaired over my reading skills; I was unable to finish reading one set of subtitles before the next one would appear. He did not hide his disappointment:

"You are rubbish… my granddad reads better than you."

Granddad suffered from Alzheimer's Disease.

Staying on the subject on reduced intellectual capacity, it may for the first long period living a foreign language country seem as if your whole brain is wrapped in Teflon. Nothing sticks. You can conscientiously read something in new world-ish and five minutes later it is totally gone – as if you had never read it before. It really is infuriating. Not only does it take ten times as long to read the damn thing in the new language, but you also have to read it five times for it to sink in. During a friendly chat you can be asked about a conversation that you had at a dinner party two days ago and you will have absolutely no recollection of it.

A vague expression of bemusement can be detected on your new world friend's face: "Did you drink a lot that night?" "Ehh, no… I just suffer from immigrant dementia."

Another symptom of this condition is the bewildering fact that names of people and places are so much more difficult to remember than those back home. It has something to do with their disconnection with childhood associations. When you meet new world X, you will have had no childhood friends who were also called X. Nothing to pin the new name to in your over-worked brain. In the old world when meeting new people their names are often familiar and you may remember someone from your past with the same name. Using this person from your past as a kind of bookmark is an efficient way of streamlining the recall process. You cannot use that technique abroad.

It is important in all societies to remember peoples' names. It makes people feel appreciated and at ease with you if you bother to remember their names. It is therefore worth the extra effort it takes to remember the difficult, foreign names.

Once working as a locum GP in Norway I visited an old man suffering from terminal cancer in his home. It was clear that he did not have long to live. The following day I was called at 11 am by a trembling voice introducing herself as the night-nurse. She told me that the old man was no longer breathing and had no pulse. Weary after a long night on call I irritated asked the night-nurse what she believed his condition to be if there indeed were no pulse and no respiration.

"Yes, hmmm… I think he must be dead then."

"Bravo, marvellous thinking. I shall be there to certify him later, good bye" I responded rudely and hung up.

On my way to the old man's isolated farm it did briefly cross my mind that it was odd that a night-nurse should be calling me at midday, and that this particular night-nurse had seemed so extremely insecure for a professional. It unfortunately had its reasons!

I walked into the farmhouse expressing my sympathy to the distraught wife that I had met the previous day. Next to her a young woman was sitting quietly supporting the old woman. As the young woman introduced herself, I, with a shiver, realized that her Christian name sounded exactly like the words "night-nurse". She was not the night-nurse. She was in fact the old man's grand-daughter. I felt nauseous as I recalled how bad-mannered I had been on the phone to her. While trying to recover my composure I apologized profusely while trying to explain the reason for my impertinence. My explanation never took off. But in some merciful way I think my stupid faux pas counted for little on this sad day for the two Norwegian women.

Force yourself to employ the new language in as many different situations as possible; listen to the radio and downloads, watch television, read books, magazines, newspapers. Most importantly of all, speak to the new world people in their own language, even if

89

they speak your language (did you get that, you anglophones?).

In a few selected instances it is clearly of value to continue to use your own language; talking to the cat, cursing yourself on the tennis court and swearing at your new world mother-in-law while you are smiling politely. It is an excellent outlet for all kinds of s/m-orbid ideas that would not otherwise find their way to the surface.

As a testament to how cocooned you can become in the conviction that your old world language is entirely your own, I have personally on a few memorable occasions discharged bodily winds in the company of unsuspecting, new world others in the absurd belief that that would go as unnoticed as my old world mutterings. Unfortunately, these "vowels" are met with a distinct global recognition that can leave the defendant pretty red-faced.

Do think while you are talking
It can be quite frightening to feel how the level and sophistication of your thoughts deteriorate for a period while you are learning the new language. The reason for this is the intimate relationship between thoughts and language that at the initial stages of emigration can feel broken. That thoughts to a very large extent *are* language is at no time more painfully evident than when you have recently plunged into the wild seas of a new language. Things you want to say, emotions you want to express, never reach their destination, because by the time you have figured out what you wanted to say, the conversation has already moved on to something completely different. And even your private thoughts do not reach past, dizzy heights due to what seems like a cerebral meltdown. It is intensely

frustrating. Your thoughts and sentiments appear to be imprisoned behind the solid bars of your linguistic inadequacies.

You feel like tearing out your hair and beating somebody up; serious symptoms of the emotional constipation that can be caused by language difficulties.

It is said that we only become ourselves by telling our stories - that all we really are, is our stories, our narratives. That story can change dramatically when told in a foreign language. Suddenly your punch carries no more sting than that of a fly. Especially if your vocabulary is hovering around 20 to 30 words, incorrectly pronounced! Pieces of our story may get lost in translation, for better or for worse.

Another problem is that words, even the ones you think you understand, do not always mean what they are supposed to mean. The cultural slant of certain expressions can totally change the meaning of what people are trying to tell you. In my adopted country, England, people, well, mainly women actually, talk a lot about firemen. For the first couple of years the connotations totally past me by. In this country firemen are supposed to be particularly sexy for women to look at. Firemen in Denmark – unfortunately for them – have no such reputation in spite their equally heroic, hose-wielding activities. A working knowledge of these kinds of culture specific idioms will add extra dept to your language. This can only be achieved by avid exposure to the new world language by listening, reading and speaking at any given opportunity. If you stick to your guns and keep speaking the new language things will improve faster than you had ever imagined at the beginning.

An American friend having lived in Paris for 25 years always says when asked about how it felt to have achieved mastery of the French language: "It was nothing less than a bloody miracle." The word "miracle" these days pronounced more the French than the English way.

It may seem unachievable to you but several authors have actually managed to switch language at an advanced age and write beautiful novels in the new tongue. Milan Kundera and Thomas Mann are examples of authors that were forced to leave their native countries, Czechoslovakia and Germany respectively, because of repressive regimes. Kundera who now lives in Paris has a different writing style in French compared to the books his has written in exuberant Czech. In French he is more economical with his words, his syntax minimalist, but still unmistakably himself. Shakespeare believed that brevity was the soul of wit. Kundera seems to have been required to use a new language before he realized that Shakespeare was right.

The new world reception that your linguistic efforts will get can largely be divided into two groups:

One group will frown and get a strained look in their faces almost before you have opened your mouth. They will look down with a vague shake of their head – while you are still mid-sentence - and declare that they really do not understand what you are saying. The most ignorant will maybe even turn to fellow new worlders and declare, usually in third person, that they have not got clue about what "he/she" is trying to say. However exasperating for the newcomer trying his heart out to talk new worldish, the comments are rarely meant in a demeaning way. It is more likely to be a manifestation of the new worlder's own lack of worldliness than his disdain for you and your efforts.

The other group will be perennially encouraging and on a regular basis let you know how amazing they find it that you are actually functioning in a foreign tongue.

The group usually consists of the more enlightened and well travelled new worlders some of whom have been abroad themselves. But the problem is their reticence towards giving you any negative feedback on your language. Only the most sophisticated members of this group will know how to give you a fair blend of encouragement and education.

Feeding back to the new worlders which approach you prefer is not an easy task but a necessary one. It must be said that there undoubtedly are cultural differences. Some cultures are more dismissive and less tolerant, while others will be more prepared, or used to, accepting differences and minor communication problems. The lesson learned can determine which stamp you will leave on your old world society's level of acceptance once returned from your travels.

Language problems can be infuriating and shake your confidence dramatically. Working in the hospitals I have on many occasions, when my tongue twisted the wrong way around some foreign verbs, felt that I was treating the poor patients as guinea pigs for my own ends. For a second, my general incompetence could seem so glaringly obvious to myself that no excuse in the world would suffice. I would start to question even my most basic skills, as giving an injection, taking blood etc. It helped to remind myself that the demarcations between different compartments of competence can become overly porous, especially when stressed. If your confidence has been shattered in one area it can easily spread like wildfire to others. The contrary is fortunately also the case when our confidence has been boosted. In both instances the change in confidence – perhaps apart from the specific, afflicted area - has little foundation in reality.

Do not deprive yourself of one of life's great joys; improving your language. In some ways it is like experiencing the toddlers' playful acquisition of verbal communication over again. They are not shy and you should not be either. Above all, do not worry about embarrassing yourself. Learning new languages is not a game that lends itself to perfectionism. There will be times where you inadvertently put your foot in it in a massive way; lacking refinement, missing hints or believing you cracked a really good joke – and being the only one that laughed. Opening your mouth becomes an ordeal, a bit like exhibiting a piece of art you have worked on for a long time to the public for the first time. You feel at the mercy of the critics - nowhere to hide. Wherever you go, the language will follow you - every time you speak you expose yourself to the judgment of others. But always remember that you are the courageous one, trying your very best in another language.

Chances are that your conversation partner knows a lot less about your language than you do about his.

As young man travelling around the USA with friends from my Copenhagen medical school we spent some days with an elderly couple north of New York. Mr. and Mrs. T were both retired dentists and they had years earlier been hosts for one of my travel companion's gap year abroad. The very distinguished Mrs. T had cooked us a lovely dinner that was also attended by the couple's seven grown-up children and their wives and husbands. I wanted so badly to be the polite boy from Europe so I said to Mrs. T:

"What a wonderful cock you are, Mrs. T."

An ominous silence abruptly fell upon the table. People stopped eating and started staring at me. The silence became so bad that Mr. T had to start clearing his throat loudly to at least fill the unbearable vacuum with some kind of sound. I sensed I had done wrong.

My brain was working overtime to come up with a solution to why things had turned out as they had around the dinner table. I finally came up with the brilliant idea that Mrs. T had drilled one too many teeth in her life and thereby suffered a loss of hearing. To rescue the situation I therefore reiterated in a louder and clearer voice:

"What a wonderful cock…"

I think that Mrs. T and the astounded family kind of understood at that point that they were dealing with a linguistic retard rather than a little pervert. The Danish translation of the word cook is spelled and pronounced "kok". I was still at the second repeat performance, totally oblivious to what all the fuss was about while the conversation grindingly took off again. My friend that had spent a year in America seemed to be doing a lot of coughing into his napkin that evening.

The more proficient with the language you become, the easier life in the new world will get; education, seeking jobs, seeking partners and simply managing to put words on your thoughts and thereby avoid a nagging feeling of dissatisfaction. The process of putting words on thoughts is clearly one of the key elements in therapy for people suffering from mental distress. Living abroad can in some ways be seen as a distressing situation. Contact with other people is in actual fact therapy in its purest form. But the tool you need to participate in human contact is language – needless to say that the more sophisticated it is the more you, and others, will benefit. You can build up a healthy competition with other immigrants, or failing that with yourself, by learning new expressions, clever syntax and proverbs in your new world language. An Italian footballer (and later manager) consistently came up with at least one new expression at the weekly after-match press conference during his stay in England. One week his team had "crossed the Rubicon" the next week he believed that "one should not count the chickens before they are hatched". It may seem artificial but it is a great way of advancing your prime instrument to improve your chances of a better stay.

Oddly enough, continuous work on your mother tongue is equally important. Some people who feel inferior about their background will refrain from speaking their native language in public, or in extreme cases even at home, in fear of being judged.

I have heard people proudly announcing that their mother tongue by now is a little 'broken'. Others, sometimes as a conscious statement, but more often out of habit, would let their native language be heard in public very, very loudly. No doubt which of these two groups will learn the new world language the fastest, but a balance has to be found that allows both languages to thrive not in spite of each other, but because of each other.

This balance was not found in the following example from our trip across the USA those many years ago. Speaking your own language abroad can backfire in more than one way. A record shop in down-town San Francisco in the mid-eighties provided the unlikely backdrop for one of the most embarrassing episodes in my adult life. Confidently browsing through the new records on sale, a friend of mine and I caught sight of a beautiful, mix-raced young girl standing next to us. My friend said to me in Danish:

"She is quite dishy, don't you think?"

"Yeah, but she is too young for us," I replied.

"Well, I don't think so… at least her legs are pretty hairy," he said.

"Gosh, you are absolutely right," I said looking down the poor girl's legs.

At that moment this anything but Danish looking girl turned around and said without the slightest rancor or accent in Danish;

"You know what, guys, I am actually 18."

Without further discussion we spinelessly turned on our heels and sprinted out of the shop as fast as our legs could carry us. Speaking a small language does not safeguard you against these kinds of mishaps. And if you, Miss mix-race, Danish lady reads this now almost 20 years on, please forgive us. The bottom line was that we thought you were pretty, but we did admittedly have a rather strange way of expressing it. When you lose, do not lose the lesson. This lesson was not lost on me and I shall carry it to my grave.

A language cannot be learned decently without making a serious stab at understanding the political and historical background of a country. It may seem a little boring to a young traveller but it is essential if you want to benefit maximally from your stay. In many big cultures, like for example the French and the British, there are excellent, manageable books which will acquaint you with these countries' history at a glance. Following the news and reading the newspapers, as best you can, will before long allow you to get a better grip of both language and culture. Soon, by reading and in discussion with locals, you will be able to pick up on references, important names and allusions that not long ago were a closed land to you. This immersion in the foreign culture will go a long way not only to restore your confidence but also to increase the enjoyment of your stay.

Do find a place to stay with a minimum of facilities

It may not be appropriate, immediately after emigrating, to find a permanent home for obvious reasons of uncertainties about jobs, length of stay etc.

But as soon as preliminary decisions have been reached about these questions, finding a quality place to live is paramount. Spending a little bit more money can make the difference on how you, a long time from now, will look back on your experiences as an expatriate. It does not need to be grandiose by any stretch of the imagination, but it needs to be yours. Put up pictures, buy plants and put your name on the door. Bring a few cherished items from your old world home to remind that all ties have not been broken. Make it homey. Make it your cave to where you can retrieve when the demands of the new world exceeds your energy level. You may in times of trouble experience an excessive need for orderliness in your new quarters. This would come as a quite a shock to one's mum. But she can be brought back to reality by the fact that this is a natural development in some one struggling to find familiar patterns and neatness in the outside world. This desire will fade again once the anxiety has dwindled. Having your own territory, however small, has never been more important.

Once you have found a place you can call home, buy a map. Orientate yourself as much as you can; find out where the public transport is, where the supermarket is, how do I get to work/school. It will immediately make you feel less lost and will furthermore improve your standing with the locals considerably. If you know certain place names and can orientate yourself it will be yet another overt sign of your commitment to the new world. A practical sense of knowing your way around the new world will give you a sense of ownership, or at least, co-ownership.

Do be confident and proud…

…of who you are and where you are from, wherever you are from. Confidence is an intangible feeling of trust in yourself *and* in people around you. I am by no means advocating a mindless celebration of all things different, but having a strong base in your own culture is the best way of making sure that the flowers of your new culture are able to put down roots. Showing that you are at ease with your background and who you are will ease your way into the new society. If you are from the humblest of backgrounds your current status will just show how far you have come! While diversity should be encouraged, inter-human communality must never be forgotten. One of the most amazing, universal aspects of human behaviour is how we inadvertently mirror each other. If you approach the new world in an anxious, frightened manner most people that you meet will respond in a similar manner. Fortunately, the same is the case if you are confident and open.

You will need a certain degree of resilience to get you past the initial rebuffs. Do not make generalisations about national character traits following a single unpleasant situation. The history of long term traveling is littered with examples of curmudgeonly emigrants who believe that the new world is only out to get them. It will not only make your stay more disagreeable but also lower your chances of success at whatever you are doing both socially and professionally.

Some people appear ashamed of their origin. This is not a new trend. The Duke of Wellington, with reference to his Irish background, claimed that "one is not necessarily a horse just because one was born in a stable". So much for pride in your origin. In spite of the Duke's undeniable success in life – he was not only victorious against Napoleon at Waterloo, he was also a distinguished statesman including a short spell as Prime

Minister of Britain – his strategy cannot be recommended. Too often have I seen people especially from poor countries become visibly uncomfortable when asked simple questions like "where do you come from?"

Look at it from another angle. People from unprivileged backgrounds have covered so much more ground to get to where they are now than people who were handed it all on a plate. That bears evidence of a hard working, tenacious attitude. Stand up for where you come from. Do not let the new world be in any doubt that you are aware of your origin and that you will stand by it while being open for new input. Being confident and having a consistent set of transcendent values will earn you much more respect. Not to mention self-respect.

Do make sure that you have something to offer...

...the new community. The good captain Cook would probably have been killed way before his eventual death in Hawaii if it had not been for his lavish gifts to the locals.

Gifts in the material sense are however not what I would suggest. In most cases a friendly and industrious attitude is sufficient. You must ensure that the locals get the impression that you are not there to sponge of them but that you have something valuable to offer society. Your contribution may initially just be friendliness and interest in their society. Lending an ear to the locals' stories - personal or about their area - will get you a long way. Showing commitment to the new world is vital and it is not a betrayal in any way to the life you left behind.

On the contrary, a committed immigrant will eventually be able to return as a fuller and richer person that will have more to offer the old world.

Having a profession or a craft is obviously always advantageous. Do not hide the fact that you have worked or studied before, and that you in due course will do the same in the new world. Acquiring the equivalent of your qualifications back home can be a bureaucratic nightmare but it usually is possible and worth the trouble. Do not feel dispirited by having to work below your normal level in the new world while you are waiting for things to be sorted out. It is not a bad way into the system that may work differently from your own.

Do be genuinely interested

Few other attitudes open doors so convincingly as genuine interest in other peoples' life and culture. Having the human surplus to ask about their life, opinions and ways of dealing with common issues will make people feel cherished and valued. Indulge yourself in local food, customs, and language. Cherish differentness. Differentness will in most cases, even when it appears to be an unwanted obstacle, end up being an addition to your personal repertoire.

If you are ever worried about forgetting your own background, taking the plunge into a new culture will paradoxically leave you with a much enhanced sense of the culture you left behind. Sometimes it feels like trying to push a jigsaw piece that does not fit into a space. You become acutely aware of the differentness. The encounter with an alien culture makes your own almost physically palpable. And you learn that you can not only live with it but also grow because of it.

Learning about new cultures cannot be done in a better way than through locals' friendship. Do not expect to find them within the confines of your room! Get out and actively seek people's company.

You will find that the more you learn about a subject the more interesting it becomes. That goes for cultures as well as human narratives. There are about seven billion of them out there and no time to waste!

Chapter IV

Immigration

"Was, wenn Vervandlung nicht
ist dein dränger Auftrag?"
(What else is there, if transformation is not
your pressing task?")

Rainer Maria Rilke

Inner scales

From the very day you set foot in the new world an inner pair of scales will occur in your mind's eye. On these scales will go all experiences of your new life. On one side will be placed what the old world had to offer, on the other side the new world's assets. The balance of the scales and what is assessed as negative and positive are based on the individual's past. It is very far from scientifically accurate but rather built on a personal logic not always understandable to others. The scales are there forever and cannot be undone, not even after returning home for good to the old world. An unending, inner tug of war has started.

It may appear annoying, but in actual fact, immigration has given you the gift of grace, the gift of comparison. Suddenly, you can hold up tangible and less tangible items in the strong light now coming from two directions and compare. Nevertheless, your old world, or rather your perception of the old world, will always be the yardstick by which any new world will be measured.

Nationhood

One of the prices you will pay for immigration can be the loss of sense of nationhood. It is a tragic loss to many immigrants who will end up using a disproportionate part of their lives attempting to restore it, either by rejecting the old world completely or launching into a mindless worship of the lost world; supporting the old world, local or national football teams, refusing to learn new world language to "honour" the old world etc. It will always be fake but it can give you brief moments when ancient bonds appear to have been mended. Accepting that a part of our minds, or perhaps more precisely our hearts, will always be assigned to the old world without being overly romantic about it, is a step in the right direction. Under no circumstance should attempts to restore old world nationhood undermine your integration efforts in the new world.

I have a black friend who lived his first 4 years in a small African country before coming to England where he has now been for 40 years. His accent is southern English, his manners are very English, his wife is English, his kids are English, he *is* a very English man. But still he suffers from what he describes as divided loyalties. As a child he would never know which cricket team to support; England, because he lived here, the West Indies, because they were black or Zimbabwe because it is close to his native country. He could never muster quite the same enthusiasm as the other kids when England was playing some sport. A few, humiliating racist experiences in his early life surely did not help either.

His case illustrates how many immigrants feel even after having lived more than half their lives abroad. It does however not cover the whole group of immigrants. Some become more – bordering to the pathological – patriotic either about the new or the old world. Which way they swing seems of less importance as long as the unequivocal allegiances provide them with a solid sense of identity. A state of mind with divided loyalties reflects an honest uncertainty that will not be "cured" by categorical viewpoints – circumstances so beautifully described in Rudyard Kipling's "The two-sided man" built on his own experiences in India and England.

Monster-making

It is easy to fall into the trap of belittling the new world in an almost obsessive manner. A Scottish colleague of mine during my Paris stay had almost made a life out of berating France and the French after having lived in Paris for more than seven years. His constant ranting and raving about the stupidities of the pauvres francais was driving everybody in the hospital up the wall.

His tirades against "frogs" were usually followed by an unsubtle suggestion from whoever was unfortunate enough to be listening that he should maybe consider going back to where he came from. When he finally did so his life - according bulletins from the Highlands – ran out of steam and he shortly afterwards had to retire on medical grounds with a bad back, an ailment that had never bothered him in France.

It seems so surprisingly natural to speak ill of your new countrymen. The differences between them and you are constantly on your mind. The meeting with the newness takes up an enormous part of your conscious thoughts. If things for some reason do not appear to go your way it takes a strong mind not to jump to the most flagrant explanation: "It must be those bastards and their bloody culture (…or usually lack of it according to the truculent newcomer) that are the cause of all my problems," ranging from lack of professional advancement to bad weather.

A coping mechanism

Being on the attack continuously concentrates the mind on the exterior world and thereby opportunely spares the aggressor the sight of his own, inner workings. Total rejection of the new world also conveniently prevents any (further?) disappointments. If you have nil expectations you have thereby created a comfortable safety cushion against unfulfilled expectations, a destructive win-loose situation. It is possible that immigrants as a group are more hypersensitive to disappointments than the indigenous population. This was maybe one of the reasons why they got up and left the old world in the first place.

The creation of external monsters, monster making, is a dangerous coping strategy for anyone living abroad. It obviously alienates the immigrant from his host society and even from any ex-pat community he may belong to. The condemnation can be so obsessional, as it did in my Scottish colleague's case, that it becomes the person's whole *raison d'etre*. It ultimately deprives the monster- maker from understanding what his own contribution to the situation may be. Denigration of others is usually – if not invariably - linked with low-esteem, a sense of feeling threatened and sometimes even depression.

Being aware of this pitfall seems to me to be one of the single most essential insights for the newcomer who has been in the new world for a period of months to years. The monster making alone can upset the entire process of integration. It is not difficult to imagine how the new world people feel about relating to a newcomer with this negative mindset. The subsequent rejection is only going to confirm the newcomer's worst expectations. A vicious circle has been established. Because it deflects any unpleasant introspection it can easily become entrenched. Nothing is more heartbreakingly pathetic than an old settler that still explains any mishaps in his life by the mere existence of the particular new world nation he settled in years previously.

Language

No excuse should prevent you from throwing yourself wholeheartedly into the battle of learning the local language as soon as you can, as well as you can. In my time abroad and at home I have heard many explanations (i.e. excuses) for why immigrants have not got around to learning the language. Let me mention a few just to make sure you will not fall into the same trap.

"Everybody understands my old world language here, why should I bother learning their language?"

Because you will never get under the skin of these new world people if you do not try. It is like walking past a treasure house daily for years without having the key to open it. Or like having a half-broken key that most of the time does not work – and even if it does, the door still does not open sufficiently and you will have to kick it in to get it open. The residents of the house do not to take kindly to that kind of brutality. The house is full of all the riches of human contact and foreign cultures, but because you cannot be bothered to learn the language, you cannot have any of it. It is a great loss and to put it crudely you have not lived abroad, in the real sense of living, until you have seriously attempted to learn the language.

It is amazing how your enhanced sense of vulnerability can be diminished when your language skills improve. A bit like equipping yourself with not only a key, but also both a sword and a shield – should you need it. You are no longer the defenseless, little foreigner that can be dragged around by his nose because he does not understand.

"My husband speaks the language fluently. He has only got a two year contract here – for me it is not worth the effort to learn the language. I can do the shopping by pointing and talking old world-ish to my fellow old world neighbours."

That policy is the direct route to clinical depression and massive phone bills back to the old world. The calls are usually repetitive in nature and consist of tearful phrases like: "Mum, I really miss you and dad *so* much…".

Not knowing the language will leave you very vulnerable and lonely. You will inadvertently create an invisible prison with glass walls where you cannot hear others and they cannot hear you. It is not uncommon that people become so isolated that they can see no other option but to return to the old world in a defeated state of mind.

Keep going

But even following years of sustained effort to learn the new world language, you are often left with a sinking feeling of still being linguistically below par. It is almost unavoidable if your first serious stab at learning the new language is after puberty. Especially, group situations are not easy to negotiate with people talking left, right and centre. This is actually also an experience frequently described by people hard of hearing, which indicates that group situation requires more linguistic capacity than one to one conversations. Not being so fast with jokes and small talk as in your own language is also common. Like most other things in life – it can be improved by practice even after years of living away from home.

Infuriatingly, new world people will still laugh and ask me to repeat certain words or phrases because it sounds "so sweet". Considering all the blood, sweat and tears you have given to reach this level of the new world language it can give you an ache to kick in their teeth and then see how sweet they will sound pronouncing the same words and phrases.

I personally still feel slightly sidetracked with the English language if people speak with heavy accents, like Scottish, Irish and Welsh. Very recently a new male nurse on ward, originally from County Durham (in North east England), told me that he had been working in Linden for a time. I nodded and smiled while my brain was working hard to place Linden on my inner map of England. I felt that I should know most of the more significant places in England after eight years in the country. But I still had no idea which town he was talking about. He proceeded to ask me if I had been there much. Bugger. "Never", I had to admit. He looked as if I was a complete cretin and asked me how long I had been in this country. I told him that I had been here for eight years where after we were cut off by some urgent patient management stuff. The following day a young, local nurse student, who had witnessed the conversation, came up to me and timidly asked if it really could be true that I in eight years never had visited London.

I spared her the real explanation that her older colleague clearly had a pronunciation problem that needed surgical intervention and told her instead that I was scared of crowds. London is an hour and fifteen minutes away from our hospital.

Wrong number
Another problem that I share with many immigrants is writing down phone numbers reeled off quickly over

110

the phone. During my stay in the London hospital I was advised to take up personal therapy with a private psychoanalyst in order to put myself in a better position to move into the next stage on the career ladder. This was a big commitment, both personally and financially, as it is not uncommon to stay in this kind of therapy for years seeing your therapist 3-5 times a week. A friendly, older consultant called me and suggested a few analysts that he knew had vacancies. It has to be said that he was, even for a native language user, a very fast speaker. I was grateful for his advice and not wanting to take more of his precious time I swiftly ended the conversation without further ado.

Nervously, I called the first gentleman on the list. His introduction sounded friendly and warm and I immediately started to spill the beans about whom I was and why I wanted to see him.

After a few minutes I paused but the analyst was still quiet. I was thinking, well, that is always the way analysis is. Long pauses are common to allow the patient to engage with their free association of thought. So, on I went about childhood traumas, broken relationships, secret desires etc.

Finally, the analyst cleared his throat while I was mid-sentence explaining about my nightly dreams of teddy bears being torn to pieces and stamped on by angry looking women in latex outfits. "You know what, mate, I am afraid that this is more than we can help you with here at Haines Electrical Devices... but I really found it interesting... which hospital did you say you were calling from?"

Now I always make people repeat phone numbers twice before I let them hang up on me.

You are the hero

Not expressing yourself as eloquently as you want to can be devilishly frustrating. It can appear as if some new world people speak deliberately slowly to you and give you menial tasks "according" to your language level. You may even have a sneaky feeling of new world people patronizing you and not taking you seriously because of your language. It can all add to a chronic sense of inferiority.

If that makes you work harder on your language, good, if it makes you give in, reconsider. Never forget that you have your own language which you master better that the vast majority of new world people master any language. You are the conquering hero whose brave acts are not readily recognized by ignorant people around you. Remember that *you* could be focusing unduly on your language, while that may not be seen as a problem from the outside. Keep going and you will improve further – even from the so-called plateau that many long-term immigrants have resigned themselves to have reached. There is no such thing as a language plateau apart from plateaux of despair or complacency. Languages – even our mother tongue – are never ending peaks that can be climbed further until the day we die.

Advantage Mr. Immigrant

Being slightly linguistically impaired certainly also has its advantages. In a room full of people talking away in new world-ish I have noticed that it is possible to shut it out and concentrate on a book or what I am writing much more effectively than if the language was my own. This is again not unlike the person with hearing problems. On many an occasion, from exams to public speaking engagements, the dictum "Oh, what is that called now in English....?" has saved me from the embarrassment of declaring that there was a glaringly big gap in my factual knowledge completely unrelated to language. Deceptively leaving people with the impression that you would have known if it had only been in your own language is not nice... but there must be some perks for us poor immigrants.

Names, as mentioned earlier, merit a whole chapter on their own. Leaving your foreign name over the phone can result in so many shenanigans that it is truly unbelievable. I have been pushed right to the edge of despair by the number of times I have been called Hans Larsen, Henson, Hassan, Hanson, Henderson or other exotic variations on the utterly trite Danish name of Hansen. I liked Dr Handsome the best.

Name calling
The whole business of names can become such an obsession that people will go to great trouble to change them. Hollywood actors of foreign origin and many others have often changed their names in order to appear more naturalized. Interestingly, it is usually immigrants from 'lower ranking' countries in the merciless international hierarchy that allow themselves to be stripped off their previous names. You do not often find an American banker living in Kenya obsessively trying to convince the authorities that taking an African name is a good idea. I have had perfectly competent friends who were fearful that if their names were mentioned they would be judged on that alone. In many cases these people have lived most, or even their entire, lives in what they still perceive to be new world.

A very clever woman of eastern European origin who attended medical school in Copenhagen could not wait to get married to a Dane and be able to write S. Jensen on her CV, thereby not revealing her foreign background. She had been in Denmark since the age of three. Often I see my patients or new colleagues starring at my name badge and listening to my accent, itching to ask where I am from. With my dark looks I think many may believe that I come from one of those above mentioned lower ranking countries. They therefore often refrain from asking in case I should feel offended about having been "found out" that I am not English. I would not.

Names of reference

Just after my arrival in the UK I worked in a psychiatric hospital on the south coast where I was approached by a young man on the locked ward. He went straight into my path and took a good, long look at me. I was, to put it mildly, not too at ease with this big, strong guy eying me up like that. So I asked in the calmest voice possible: "Hi, how are you?"

He answered: "How I am does not matter at all, because you are Thomas the Tank Engine... or at least, you look exactly like him."

I happily agreed – "Ahh, yes...eh, well spotted, my young friend."

I quickly circumvented the young man and made my way to the nurses' station to ask a local nurse who the hell Thomas the Tank Engine was. She laughingly explained that he was children's cartoon figure, a steam train with an eternally smiling face at the front.

I was not amused! The young guy must have been very psychotic to make that link and I had to work mightily hard to quell an instant and strong desire to "review" (i.e. increase) his medication there and then. The story illustrates how different frames of references can hamper true communication. If I had known whom Thomas the Tank Engine was in the first place I would have run the patient over on the spot.

In all seriousness, knowing children's literature, songs and television programmes gives an extra insight into a society and allows you to understand references and allusions in everyday new world life that are denied to most foreigners. Just think about how many comments that you make referring to childhood memorabilia in the company of old world people. These early experiences actually make up a very important ingredient of people's sense of national affiliation. Being a walking encyclopedia on *Winnie the Pooh* has the added benefit of giving you the edge should you ever enter into a heated debate with 8-year olds about the true nature of Tigger and the Owl. And do not worry, after a little while, children quite like odd people like us with funny accents and different looks, though they often find it difficult to comprehend how you possibly could have missed the vital, last episode of the Tele-Tubbies.

False friends
Even for immigrants with a good level of the new world language, "false friends" (the French call them faux amis) are always something to be on the look out for.

The list of examples is long and embarrassing. I have already entertained you with my slip up between the Danish "kok" (meaning 'cook') and the English "cock". But also more mundane words such as e.g. successful, middle class, smart, chauvinistic and philosophical in English and the words nerveux and confus in French have caused me trouble. Although direct equivalent words exist in my native language Danish, the words do not mean exactly the same. These subtle differences remain hidden even for many expert language users. The only way out is to ask the locals then and there if they seem slightly bemused about something you have just said. Personally I did not even have to ask when in Paris, keen to make an impression, I told a young lady that I thought that both she and her flat were "tres luxurious". Unfortunately luxurious in French is not what is seems. In both Danish and English it means grand, top of the range. In French it means horny.

Homesickness – and how to deal with it
Homesickness (HS) is a state of mind characterized by prolonged longing for a previous phase in your life. It is often associated with fluctuating mood, intrusive images and recurrent thoughts of people, relationships and conditions in the old world, intermittent insomnia, poor concentration, self-reproach, guilt and maybe even reduced appetite and weight-loss. There is usually some reduction in the ability to function.

Some degree of symptoms can be encountered in almost all travellers and emi-/ and immigrants. The lack of familiarity, a strong sense of not belonging and being overwhelmed are usually present in people with HS.

There are certain risk factors for protracted HS: sudden, involuntary removal from home soil, very young immigrants, introverted personalities. Being very close to your family is, surprisingly enough, not a risk factor, but rather an indication that you also will be able to create meaningful relationships abroad.

HS usually starts before we even take off from the old world. Unlike conventional HS, which diminishes in intensity with the passage of time, anticipatory HS increases as the leaving date becomes imminent. Interestingly, as the obligatory rounds of good-byes build up, you may start to feel the urge to get it over and done with in a hurry. Saying goodbye can be quite draining. On the other hand, the intensity of the intimacy that can be experienced in the period leading up to departure can be a heartening reminder that life is worth living.

Confront your fears

If the would-be emigrant caves in to the inevitable temptation to call it all off and stay at home, the anticipatory HS has won and has simultaneously changed your relationship with the old world forever. The old world will thereafter be perceived through different glasses. Some manage to appreciate more what they thought could have been lost, while others - the majority - start to resent the old world. This resentment probably has its origin in externalized guilt caused by never actually having completed a project that had received so much emotional investment. This theory is corroborated by the sometimes flagrant banality of the excuses that are given by failed emigrants; "who was going to feed the cat... I can't live without the kind of cheese that the corner shop is doing." Most of the excuses are down to a terror of unleashing the ugly beast of fear of being on unfamiliar ground.

This beast has opportunely been hidden away in a cupboard called comfort zone. The beasts of fear feast on comfort zones resulting in those zones becoming ever narrower. If the fear is not confronted the ratio of deeds dared to deeds not dared risks becoming infinitely small, not only with regard to traveling but with regard to all endeavours that take courage. Meaningful things take courage, without exception. The poor light in the comfort zone leaves the fear open to distortion by our imagination. The truth of the matter is that the fear – like most fears - is a lot less scary when dragged out of the dimly lit comfort zone and confronted in full daylight. Do not allow your life to be narrowed down but utilise the immense energy that is locked up in fear to take off into a future of *your* choice. The turtle can live for a hundred years because of its protective shell. It only moves forward when it sticks its head out.

It is with courage as it is with the biceps – the more it is used the stronger it gets. Immigration is a heavy dumbbell.

Three stages of HS
After leaving the old world HS can be roughly divided into three stages.

Bewilderment
Stage 1. An initial numbness and bewilderment may occur just after parting from your loved ones. Crying, strong sense of insecurity and distress often accompany a disbelief that you have actually set out on this journey. Efforts to perpetuate the lost old world are in evidence by an investment in objects that remind the homesick person of home. These "linkage objects" can be anything from family pictures to a pair of socks that your mother knitted for you when you were seven. Use of relics can be helpful in desperate moments to detach yourself from reality for a split second, not unlike the momentary reprieve that valium tablets can offer the anxious soul.

But overuse – again not unlike valium - can get in the way of straight thinking and establishing new relationships, especially if you insist on wearing the socks your mother knitted on dates with new friends and partners!

A lump in your throat reminds you of all the good things you have left behind. But not of the bad things you left behind... and not of the good things that lie ahead either.

Reality sinks in

Stage 2. In spite of constantly reliving memories of the old world, reality slowly starts to sink in. The homesick at this stage - which usually occurs days to weeks after the departure - can to the outside world appear listless, withdrawn and apathetic. The condition may fluctuate dangerously, especially on days of special importance to the immigrant such as birthdays, Christmas and anniversaries. This is not sign of malignant deterioration but rather of a sensitive soul being tested. The stage can be speeded up by human contact of any kind.

Reorganisation

Stage 3 is a phase of reorganization in which the acutely painful aspects recede. The homesick person is starting to feel like he or she is returning to life. The immigrant that has completed the different stages of HS successfully will at this stage start to hold a more balanced picture of the old world in his mind; a picture consisting of both joy and sadness. He will now have selected some old world characteristics that he would like to bring along into his new world life. It may be politeness, eagerness, dignity or a clothing style or ways of preparing food. These characteristics are traits that perhaps hitherto he had been unaware were valuable to him. It corresponds to the old American Indians carrying the head band of their dead to obtain the strength of the forefathers. This selection process automatically forces an increased understanding of which qualities are worth bringing along and which should be allowed to remain in the old world.

An appreciation that the new world life you have embarked on can be rewarding slowly starts to emerge out of the clouds of homesickness.

Under normal circumstances completion of this process takes anywhere from a month to one year depending on the individual situation, the immigrant's experience and personality make-up. Unresolved HS can result in all kinds of ailments, such as unrealistic glorification of the old world, haughty denigration of the new world (see Monster-making) and, in extreme cases, clinical depression.

The line between HS and depression can seem fine, but in reality HS rarely develops into depression. Most HS sufferers realise that their ailment is time limited, normal, and responsive to empathy and support. This is not the case in depressive individuals who more than anything else appear to have lost all hope for the future. Furthermore, the homesick person does not suffer from the depressed person's exaggerated loss of self-esteem and self-hatred.

Avoid isolation

As for remedies against HS, the avoidance of isolation seems to be the best advice available. Narrow self-absorption must be avoided at all costs as it intensifies most psychological problems. This is clearly easier said than done for the newcomer who does not know a soul in the new world. However, as mentioned elsewhere, there are ways out of this; job, sports, neighbours, fellow travelers, fellow students, bars, people in the street and parks etc. Make sure that you appear accommodating. Isolation is the highway to a dysfunctional start in your new life.

Furthermore, it is of value to make a rational analysis of what you are actually missing from home. Ask yourself if your memories of your past have become somewhat embellished by your absence. Remind yourself why you left and what you are achieving by being abroad. As with most psychological experiments the power is enhanced by talking to others or by writing it down.

Just as with valium, phone calls and especially early visits to the old world should be used only sparingly. These remedies have the same risk-profile as valium; they are addictive and they prevent you from working consciously through your problem and moving on to a more advanced stage in your life.

However it can, if not life saving then at least be 'project-immigration saving', to make a little pity-invoking phone call back home every now and again.

It is normal

The most important thing is to realize that it is an entirely normal state of affairs to feel homesick, even for adults! It would actually be directly abnormal and worrying if such feelings did not occur following a momentous event like immigration. Mourning the loss of the old world is the price paid for wining the new world - while still holding the old world in your heart.

Does HS sound like a medical condition to you? Well, in some ways it is, ignoring the fact that HS rarely needs medical intervention.

The feelings we encounter on leaving home are in so many ways akin to what we go through when we lose some one close to us. Here also no specific treatment exists, about from human company and time spent productively. The homesick also need a little dose of common sense; for the vast majority of immigrants the old world is not 'lost' in the sense that there is no way back or that everybody back home has died. Modern technology makes communication easy if you ever need proof of your loved ones' continued existence.

Transport has also developed from the days where people waved goodbye on the quay never to see each other again. In most people a degree of HS will always be there even 10, 20, or 30 years down the line, but usually to a manageable extent. On occasions, I find myself searching on the Internet for property not just in Denmark but in my childhood home town even though the chances of a speedy return are remote. I presume that is a symptom of a momentary relapse of slushy HS. The outcome of HS is, however, generally favourable, however painful the whole process may have been.

The bereaved also passes through different stages before returning to some kind of normality; not the same normality as before, though, but to a wiser and more insightful normality, despite the fact that the hurt will never disappear completely. To reach that stage is the essence of why we voluntarily go through the artificial bereavement process that immigration in reality is.

Illness

Illness is at the best of times difficult and often requires quick action and adaptation. This is never more acutely obvious than when you live far away from loved ones.

The phone in your new world can therefore become quite a dreaded device. You may often have had the thought that some day it will ring and pass on the news that you never want to hear. The thought can become so intense that in an irrational, superstitious attempt to prevent it from happening, you will be thinking the worst every time the phone rings.

The truth is that if you stay an immigrant for long enough it will happen one day - loved ones will be taken ill or will die. Thoughts of guilt and worry hit you like a tidal wave. The dormant sense of having betrayed something sacred - which has never left entirely anyway - now flares up with renewed vigour. "How could I have left these people for so long... I must take the next plane home and never return to this wretched country (i.e. new world) ever again".

It is painful if somebody important to you has been taken ill and is suffering far away without you being able to be there in person. However, it is worth realising that you would in most incidences have been unable to contribute much in practical terms even if you had been there from the onset of the illness. It is nevertheless pivotal to be there for your sick relative and offer your presence and support during periods of serious illness. And, thanks to modern aviation, that is in actual fact feasible for the majority of immigrants.

Stop feeling guilty
Arriving back home for this special occasion is an emotional time where once again things are experienced with heightened intensity. The suffering of your relative can seem to carve you up inside, and having to leave them again is soul destroying. But you do have your life elsewhere and your relative is not interested in holding you back.

It must be kept in mind that there are limitations to what you *can* do whether you are here or there. Seriously unwell people have an uncanny tendency to develop an almost serene magnanimity at least partly unrelated to their past personalities. Suddenly they appear to have raised themselves above everyday life spite and reproach. A brush with death eliminates pettiness and vindictiveness to an extent that it can alter your relationship with that person forever. Blame is rarely at the forefront of their minds.

It is advisable to prepare for these kinds of emergencies right from the beginning of your new world stay, and keep emergency funds to cater for these situations. It would not be nice to be unable to afford the trip home because you had bought tickets for a football match.

New strength

Being taken ill yourself in the new world pushes some buttons of infantile helplessness in most immigrants, even after years of having lived abroad. There is often an overwhelming urge to go home to all the things that make you feel safe. A mistrust of the new world health system is often based more on personal shock than on facts. Your capacity to cope with newness has taken a drastic battering and you will prefer the things that are familiar and which remind you of a safer period of your life. You may feel very small and lost, but if you manage to get through it you will have discovered a new dimension of your strength, and furthermore have tested out the quality of your new world network. In my experience that network is chronically underestimated by immigrants, just as the old world network can unfortunately be overestimated in the beleaguered mind of the sick immigrant.

Serious illness is never easy to handle, at home or abroad. It is fears about pain, infirmity, guilt, loneliness, death and being a burden which usually trouble our minds in moments when the body is letting us down. The distance to the safest place in your mind, your old world home, intensifies all these emotions. Overcoming these problems in a mature way is a task no one would wish for you, but once again it adds considerably to your human curriculum vitae

Settling down

Little by little a new 'everyday life' develops for the immigrant in the new world. Going to work in the morning you start to recognize the people on the bus; you know which newspaper you like to read, and you have become an integrated part of your work team and perhaps a sports club or social scene. You no longer wake up with a pounding heart unsure if you are going to make it through the day. The day may have come when you were able to give directions to a lost person in a new world street. And even be fairly sure the directions given were correct!

New normality

In spite of this apparent sense of normality, all is not normal. Everyday life abroad will never reach the same level of all-encompassing normality as back home, even if you have lived more years abroad than you have in old world. Moving to a different climate and landscape helps keeping the sense of everyday routines in your new world life at a distance. Even years down the line I can marvel at being able to go for a walk in the mountains (my old world is flat as a pancake), seeing spring blossom in March and April and experiencing winters without the Nordic darkness. And true to the inconsistency of the human spirit, I can miss cross-country skiing in a snowstorm and the cosiness of a dark, cold winter's night in front of the fire. The English radio and television weather forecasters will days in advance of a cold spell put on a stern face and warn the public about an "artic cold snap with damaging northerly winds". It usually turns out to be a bit of frost on the windscreen in the morning and a light breeze in the treetops, conditions that in Denmark would be described as spring-like. Immigrant life will never become 100 % real.

No pigeonhole fits

As an immigrant you have also somehow fallen out of the social hierarchy. You may have a job, a house and a spouse but you still do not fit into any known category. The same applies if you return home. You can no longer be pigeon-holed. It gives enormous freedom, but the usual flipside is a sense of lack of belonging to a specific group with whom you can identify and fight battles alongside.

Developing tolerance does not always come automatically. Immigrants can be very judgmental about the performance of other emi-/immigrants; scathing about their language, about the way they dress or about their level of integration, whether too little or too much. It often baffled me to experience the urge in myself to mock innocent people from foreign cultures who for some reason did not fit the bill. What bill, you may ask. Who created that bill? God knows.

I believe that the urge to belittle fellow immigrants stems from a personal sense of insecurity. It is easy to pour scorn on someone else who perhaps more overtly than you is not living up some fictitious level of perfection. It conveniently deflects attention from own shortcomings. Moreover, you hope that by 'standing on the corpses" of others your own achievements will seem more formidable compared to others who essentially belong to the same minority group, the newcomers.

It is a nasty, though partly understandable, way of dealing with feeling threatened. It is not to be recommended, not only for the sake of the poor, fellow emi-/immigrant, but also because it leaves most observers with a view of you as unsympathetic and callous. On closer inspection one will find that the communalities of humankind are obvious for those prepared to open their eyes.

On the positive side you will soon realize that things that you previously regarded as indispensable no longer appear to be that at all. The absence of certain food items, a beloved recreational pursuit, clothing items, books, the television or even certain people's company do not actually endanger your existence. New and worthwhile value systems have been shuffled into place by living else where.

It is peculiar how fellow countrymen more "senior" than yourself in the immigration game can suddenly take on the status of a sporting hero in your universe. They have tackled the hurdles that you initially have found so impossible. They seemingly have achieved so much, not unlike the picture you as a first grader had in your mind of the kids in the second grade – until you yourself were promoted to the second grade! Simply being able to discuss things you have gone through with somebody having similar experiences is of real benefit. Lifetime friendships can be made as a result of this.

The eagle has landed

Integration and more peace of mind creep up on you and are an indication that a part of you has now become new world. In spite of the slow process of integration, one day you suddenly realise that part of your brain has been freed up to do other things rather than just hanging onto life by the skin of your teeth. Suddenly, you can think of other more creative things than just surviving. The world seems wider.

The eagle has landed. That may feel quite upsetting to those who hoped to remain 100 % old world in spirit in spite of emigration. For the benefit of this group, look at it from a different perspective; the 20 % of you that after some period is now new world has been added to your personality, rather than deducted from

127

who you were before. This means that you are actually 120% of the person you were when you left. This is an achievement that deserves every form of self-congratulatory measure you can think of. Furthermore it adds to the sense of triumph if you try to think back on what seemed to be problematic, perhaps even insurmountable a year – maybe just months – ago. It is worth taking a moment from the pursuit of future goals to look back and get into perspective what you have already achieved. This is not at all to encourage complacency, but merely to suggest that a realistic look at your own achievements is productive before you attempt to overtake the future in the fast lane.

Serial immigrants
Some people will move and change country at the rate other people change their underwear. This is for example true of the diplomatic brigade that move often, and to my understanding without much say in the matter. This is a risky business, as most repetitive things are. Some doctors have labeled it dromomania (an abnormal, obsessive desire to roam). It is characterised by an addiction to high octane experiences. The reality is often very different. Constantly being on the look out for newness may be an attempt to avoid a single repetition of one experience. The determined search to avoid repetition can prove to be the exact route to it - a paradox rarely conscious to the serial immigrant. But is it really a disease, or is it rather a further extrapolation of a widespread wish to escape from ourselves? What else is there to escape from?

Longer term relationships with any others than the closest family will, to the serial immigrant, become unfamiliar territory. Even the closest family may dwindle in numbers faster than expected for the rapid mover, with children at far away boarding schools, and a spouse spending long periods in the old world. Attempts to establish deep contacts are often abandoned because the futility of it seems so obvious. They are forever in transit. They lead a sterile life with endless visits to faceless restaurants with fellow immigrants who are as easily forgotten as the restaurant. Conversations circle around the same monotonous issues – "where are you from?... it most be cold... oh, you speak many languages" ... etc. In spite of great knowledge of many foreign cultures, the gypsy lifestyle of the serial immigrant can lead to a sentiment of being a tourist in other people's lives - and ultimately in your own.

A permanent feeling of never having arrived, of constantly giving in to a nomadic impulse, makes you a wanderer. Wandering can become a personal manifesto, a solution to all problems that immediately distance you from trouble, and after a little while, from yourself. The wanderer may feel that he has unlocked the riddle of human freedom and like a rolling stone he gathers no moss, or anything else.

Irritants

It is almost impossible to steer clear of certain points of irritation in the new culture, even for the well-integrated immigrants. They can range from the way people look or dress, to attitudes and values or to ways of decorating the houses or the up-keep of public spaces.

It is interesting that immigrants often express serious irritation about these new world idiosyncrasies and forget that other idiosyncrasies, admittedly often different ones, once contributed significantly to their drive to leave their old world. As explained before, the newcomer has to open every pore to let in all the new impressions. Turning on extreme receptiveness is a necessary survival mechanism that happens more or less automatically, but it comes at a price. In taking in so much new information over a short span of time, there is bound to be some stuff that will get right up your nose. The usual filters are not working and you are defencelessly being overloaded with all things new, good and bad. The irritants are usually things that are foreign to your own culture and in some form appear over and over again.

I would love to share some of my favourite irritants with you from my eight year long stay in the UK because I have heard, that a problem shared is a problem halved!

National obsessions that are taken for granted in our own culture can stand out as absolutely, outrageously boorish and dim-witted in other cultures. To my eyes British culture thrives – among other things - on cricket, depressing soaps and a tabloid press so appallingly lowbrow that it defies description.

The soaps are based on pubs in run down inner city areas and the deprived people visiting these pubs. The acting is in many cases so atrocious that it takes the term dilettantism to hitherto unknown levels of embarrassment while the scriptwriters are constantly racking their brains to come up with yet more cunning plots to beat the record number of people watching the special Christmas jumbo edition subtitled: "How could Phil father 15 year-old Rachel's unborn child when he was shot dead two years ago?" The soaps seem to serve the sole purpose of trying to convince the lower classes that others are worse off than them, thereby preventing them from gathering to march on Buckingham Palace for a revolution. 'Soaps' are a modern opium for the people. Outsiders watching more than a few minutes of this misery risk severe, clinical depression.

Televisions can be switched off but it is more difficult to find the on and off button on your work colleagues who use their breaks to enthusiastically discuss the latest developments in this fictitious, soap pub. The fact that they are discussing these characters, that at the very best are no more than one-dimensional templates (e.g. evil-Eddie and good-Gareth) as though they were actually real people seem to pass them by completely. The mind-bogglingly stupidity of the soaps brings the nation together in passionate discussion while less than 50 % of the electorate are bothered to cast their vote at general elections!

To the ignorant eye, cricket appears to be a game where one player throws a ball and another attempts to hit it with a bat while all the others, players and audience, are bored stupid. The pale skinned English audience that happily travels across the world to follow their heroes' activities is usually rewarded by a crushing defeat and appalling sunburns as a good match should last no less than five days. An erroneous umpiring decision can cause rioting in the streets across the Commonwealth nations. My advice would be to attempt to recruit a new brigade of umpires just a shade under 90 - the approximate average age of the present lot. A small dose of televised cricket would overtake the latest scientific advances on hypnotics. Surely not even the most ardent insomniac would be able to resist the powers of cricket.

This opinion is of course not aired openly, but one's sheer lack of knowledge - and interest - in the tea-break score in the test match against the West Indies can make you feel rather isolated. The main cricket ground in the UK is by the way, modestly, called 'Lords'!

The English tabloid press is in league of its own. To my knowledge no other country's press can muster quite the same levels of profanity combined with callous exploitation of the under-classes' ignorance. On days when people have been killed in wars and important political decisions have been taken, the tabloids will clear their front pages to report on a measly little court servant's observations of royal bedchamber activities, or the marriage break-up of a soap star, or the changing hairstyles of a football player. These are all real examples. Nothing seems too low to report. As these are by far the biggest-selling newspapers in the country, one cannot help but consider that the phenomenon of tabloidism reflects not only the thinking of a few calculating as well as deranged people at editorial level, but also that of a large part of the population.

Some people will go to extremes to follow the latest development in their favourite soap or on the cricket pitch, by calling in sick at work, cancelling holidays or even their own wedding. It may, for the outsider, come across laughably empty-headed – and it did to me.

A kind of glue

But, actually these sorts of activities serve an important purpose in modern society. In the urban, busy life most of us live it gives us a certain sense of cohesion, something we have in common. In the 'old days' we could talk about the neighbours in the village or the spat about hunting rights with the next village down the road. These issues are often no longer of concern and we have frantically been looking for replacements ever since. These mundane issues are, whether we like it or not, the glue that keeps society together. Most societies however pride themselves that their particular glue is slightly different from that of other societies.

Therefore, as a foreigner, you have been given a different kind of glue as a christening gift that does not work in your new environment. You may even experience in yourself a certain reluctance to make any changes (like learning the rules of cricket or the names of soap stars). Together with language and cultural differences the fact there is a different glue is the essence of why total integration is almost impossible. Closing off and ridiculing the new world's glue in an act of defiance is perhaps a naïve gesture of loyalty towards the old world. But it can be sobering to look at your own culture's glue. You will discover that it may be different but often equally ridiculous.

Values out of necessity

You will soon learn that cultures which have a shortage of certain goods develop rules to minimize their value. In my native country of Denmark there is generally an open and relaxed attitude to sexuality and nakedness.

People are on the whole good-looking and sex is readily available to most peoples' satisfaction. Talking about sexual subjects has therefore become acceptable at dinner-parties and it takes outrageous matters like paedophilia to offend people.

Not so in the UK. Sexual subjects are pounced upon by official as well as private individuals who take pride in reeling off all the evil consequences of sexual activities; AIDS, teenage pregnancy, rape etc., while turning a blind eye to the positive results of sex: fun, intimacy between people and fulfillment of a natural urge. This is clearly an example of rules and values having been developed out of sheer necessity in a more puritanical setting.

It somehow eases the blow of not having whatever you may want, if you are able to refer to specific moral values, while ignoring that these values were developed for that very reason.

The same mechanism is at play in Denmark when it comes to achieving high social status or above average income. The progressive tax system evens out income very efficiently and it is very difficult both financially, artistically and academically to rise above the average. Danes police each other zealously to make sure that nobody gets more than they have themselves. The ones that do well become resented, the ones that do less well become resentful.

A cunning device to avoid envy is put into place: "Money is not important, why are you focusing so much on money", Danes would say. They thereby fail to see that it is they who are focusing on money because they cannot have it, just as the British who have less easy access to sex. Thus the attitude of 'sour grapes' rewritten for a larger audience.

These are very delicate issues and must be treated accordingly. They are as interesting to observe as they are imperative to be aware of them. Such values of necessity can be freely discussed with other immigrants, but should only be discussed with selected people from the host population as the potential to cause offence is enormous. In such a discussion it is important to let the new world people know that the survival mechanism of developing values of necessity is universal and not only applies to his or her country. Using your native country and their values of necessity as an example usually has a calming effect.

Transformations in time
Transformation is a mathematical operation moving objects without alteration in system of co-ordinates. Likewise, attitudes or behaviours can seem transformed

from different time periods while travelling between different cultures.

These transformations can make you think you have travelled into a different century and you sometimes have to pinch your arm to make sure are not dreaming. The politeness I have come across in Britain and, believe it or not, also occasionally in France is mindboggling for a modern Dane. Transformations in time can take many different shapes, attitudes, beliefs, ways of interacting, values, family life etc. It can be religious beliefs that appear unchanged not just for centuries but for millennia. It can of course also be more materialistic things such as transport, technology, dress code or architecture.

Some of these transformations are joyful others frustrating, but they all contribute to underline the fact that you are far away from home. They can be utterly baffling but must be negotiated with outmost tact not to cause offence. This does not mean that differences should not be discussed, but any condescending attitudes will not endear you to the locals neither will it bring forward any positive changes.

Not long ago, flying back from Norway to the UK, I was placed next to two young Norwegians on their way to Africa via London to become missionaries. Norway, and especially certain parts of Norway, is much more religious than the culture I left in Southern Scandinavia. They were highly intelligent, young university students taking a year out to spread the word amongst the poorest of the poor. They were deeply religious, did not believe in evolution, but did believe in Adam and Eve, did not believe in sex before marriage, but did believe in hell for eternity for non-believers etc. In spite of the gulf between our ways of understanding the world I could not help but liking them and their youthful enthusiasm. When they came to hear about my status as a fallen man they exchanged consecrated looks, whispered a few words to each other before the girl next to me turned around and asked me if they could pray for me.

"Pray away, my dears."

She grabbed my arm firmly and started to pray fervently for me and my wayward soul with closed eyes, rocking movements of her body and breathless mumbling. The intensity of her passions for the Cause did undeniably have some effect on my disobedient body, in all probability not the - for her - desired effect, I imagine. After about 10 minutes of heavenly bliss she finally opened her watering eyes and asked if I had felt something. I confirmed that I had indeed felt "something".

"That was the Holy Ghost" she proclaimed with a jubilant smile.

I was not so sure.

3 o'clock in New York, 1938 in London.
Your new world friends may be passionately engaged in campaigning and lobbying for some of these issues, e.g. convincing the Church of England that female vicars are really not all that bad or that fox hunting is perhaps a trifle cruel, while you have a feeling that those battles should have been won before the time of crusades. These kinds of disparaging feelings can easily drive a wedge between you and otherwise perfectly upright new world people. They may in their rosy-cheeked excitement find your disbelief and odd cynicism hard to swallow. I suppose that this was what Bette Midler meant when she said: "When it is 3 o'clock in New York City, it is 1938 in London." This leaves you in a difficult position; your communication with your new world friends about changed cultural values is difficult, while your old world friends would

have no idea what all the fuss is about. That leaves you with a pretty limited audience for your thoughts.

Islands of sanity

This is where other immigrants especially from your own culture sphere become so important. You can feel strongly drawn towards fellow immigrant countrymen – sometimes even towards countrymen that in all probability would not have interested you much back home. When contentious issues like time transformations are discussed, these people can appear like islands of sanity in choppy waters. "So, I am not going totally mad after all…"

That is one of the main reasons – along with the delight of hearing your own language spoken - why some immigrants seek fellow countrymen so desperately when living abroad. Not only frightened third world emigrants huddle together in so-called ghettos. Look at the Italians in America, the British in Spain and the Chinese everywhere. Friendships for life can be made in surprisingly little time and bonds forged in adversity are difficult to break. You can briefly fool yourselves into believing that you never really left in the first place. But you did.

Baritone and female

A little illustration of one these points was a bewildering situation I came across during my stay in London working as a junior-doctor. The consultant in charge of our post-graduate education, Dr B., was an extremely authoritarian person based at a nearby sister hospital. Throughout my year there were three or four occasions when this doctor phoned me, basically telling me in forceful terms what to do and what not to do with my postgraduate training. Following his advice I passed my exams and was told that the custom was to meet up with Dr B. and to talk about future career plans.

I duly made an appointment and made my way to Dr B.'s hospital in my Sunday best. I greeted the secretary who announced my arrival over the intercom. I entered Dr B.'s office without any delay, only to discover he was not there. Very strange. Only a middle-aged woman was sitting at the enormous desk scribbling away without looking up. I cleared my throat a couple of times without any effect and then finally asked if she had seen Dr B. She looked up over her half glasses, stared at me for a long second as if I had been an insect in her soup and then said with a deep baritone; "Young man, *I* am Dr B".

This was slightly embarrassing, but had she known that I had thought she was a man for the last 12 months, I believe there would have been a real risk of me having ended up over her knee. Her deep voice had let me to believe that she was a powerful, controlling middle-aged man. The adoption of a masculine voice is a widespread phenomenon in the UK, used by women with career ambitions. Just listen to the female news presenters who seem to be in competition over who can hit the deepest note. All in all, this is an unsuccessful attempt to appear more in charge, while all they are really doing is pandering to the male dominated society that they joined because they could not beat it. Some societies have moved on from women having to play this humiliating role. Even without deepening their voice Danish women are naturally scary! Real women issues like child care, equal pay and long working hours are not being tackled, while manufactured female music groups, like the "Spice Girls" claim that girl power has taken over. Then again, they were manufactured by men!

Biased focus

Interestingly, there are also areas were my new host society seem far ahead of what I knew from my old world. In my particular case, in the treatment of severely mentally ill people is of interest. The British method of gently attempting to understand the underlying reasons why these unfortunate people have developed their symptoms are light years ahead of the forceful approach I knew from my old world, with its huge doses of side-effect prone medication and high incidence of involuntary treatments such as medication, admission to hospital without consent and tying patients to their beds.

For some reason these progressive changes are always less in the forefront of our minds than those instances when the new world seems to lag behind that to which we were used. Perhaps it has to do with the fact that progress is easier to accept than steps backwards. Perhaps this is because we are less ready to accept faults in our old world system with which we invariably identify more than with anything in the new world. It is important to remind yourself about the fact that cultural transformations through time work both ways to achieve a fair and realistic balance in your mind.

A more serious example of the issue of transformations through time is the current conflict between the Arab world and the West. This has been called a conflict of civilizations but to a very large degree it is a conflict between different eras. Both combatant groups are unwilling to yield an inch or to embark on the 'time-travelling' that is necessary to empathize with the other. 'Time travel' is a key feature of successful integration and may well contribute to a more peaceful world.

Battle of values

The work place and the media are awash with sexual allegations of harassment and the intimate lives of famous people. "Cabinet minister's affair with prostitute" "Will is gay" "Becks is two-timing Posh". These are some of the more explicit statements of values that meet you on a daily basis in any news agent in my adopted country, the UK.

I regularly cringe and have to look away in order not to give in to a strong urge to buy that proverbial one way ticket back to my little home town in the Danish sticks.

But it gets a lot more important than that. Core issues as fundamental as how to divide the wealth of a society, how to delegate power in society, what to believe in spiritually, what is acceptable behaviour between people and many more contentious issues can make new world life challenging. These deep-seated values are probably laid down at a very early age which means that they pretty much make up your core belief system. A belief system that serves as the glasses through which you see the world. Your values can seem so obvious and indisputable that you can be seriously shaken by meeting radically different viewpoints. This meeting can create a strong, but often unarticulated sense of dissonance that can insidiously chip away on your resolve to stay in the new world.

Time keeping

Difficulties arose for me with regard to time keeping. My old world takes time keeping very seriously and woe betides anyone who tries to be late. It is seen as a sackable offence to be late more than once and people will go through fire and water to be in time for an appointment. This seemingly pedantic attitude is cleverly linked in with morality at an early stage. "You are showing disrespect to mommy for being late" the angry Danish mother waiting outside the kindergarten would say to her oblivious offspring.

Coming across different ways of looking at timekeeping can therefore be an immensely frustrating affair. Especially when your anger over late arrivals is met with an air of genuine lack of understanding in the faces of the new world people. This is an example of how the negative scan on your inner scale can gather weight very quickly and through no fault of anyone.

Be a good sport
Paradoxically, the English genuinely still swear by being a "good sport". Cheating at a sports ground is seen as entirely unacceptable and happens much less frequently than that which I was used to back home. Bending the rules – not only in sport but also in traffic – is simply not done with the same regularity as I had grown up with. Whether this is a result of harsh punishment or robot-like discipline that compromises independence and imaginative thinking, is another story. It was a real relief to come on the tennis courts, or roads for that matter, without every time having to expect a major brawl because of dodgy behaviour. It was not hard to adjust to these improved (compared to my old world) values, and after only a short while were easy to take for granted. Indeed, their absence was notable on visits home to the old world.

A more subtle example is how age is viewed. Some cultures revere their elders – noticeably poorer countries where reaching old age is seen an achievement – while in other countries – usually the rich, developed countries – see old people as a burden which needs to be put away in care homes. That obviously creates ample ammunition for conflict. So much for the much-heralded globalization of values.

Sometimes it even comes to open conflict between two different value systems. Again the principle of 'choosing your battles with care' applies. It is usually a case of 'you against all the others' and it takes a very tenacious personality to stand your ground. It should not however prevent you from discussing matters, and you will find you will be able to sharpen your arguments in healthy discussions.

Frankly, these values are not going to change radically for most grown-up people during their new world stay. This is not the case for more peripheral values, e.g. what is acceptable to eat, when to go to bed, what to wear, which can all cause some consternation on returning to the old world.

An explanation of home-grown terror

A build up frustration due to irritants and battles of values may make you wish bad things to happen to the new world, such as defeat in sports, a collapsing economy or things that are much worse, such as death and destruction of the inhabitants. The world wide terrorist efforts bear grim evidence of the latter; many of the terrorists are people brought up in western societies with a very serious axe to grind. We have yet to discover exactly how this hatred came about, but a sense of alienation and humiliation undoubtedly played a part. They may also feel that their values have been disregarded or even ridiculed by their new world country. Many host country people will not accept this explanation and feel bitterly betrayed by the "enemy within". They feel they have nourished a cuckoo in their nest that has now turned on them and spread destruction all around. This was very much the understandable reaction of the people after London bombings in July 2005 and the Boston bombings in April 2013.

This is of course an extreme example that is as pathological as it is hideous. But is not uncommon to hope for minor unpleasantness to be endured by the host nation, ranging from financial misfortune to defeat on the football pitch. Sharing these wishes with new world people is not recommended. It can turn even the most passive new world person into a raging nationalist.

To wish for the downfall of the new world can be the product of an unhealthy obsession with the negative sides of immigrant-life. It signals that a re-evaluation of your reasons to stay or go is overdue.

Relationships

Immigrants often complain bitterly about the loss of old world friends. There is no denying that long term absence make friendships fall by the wayside. It is also beyond doubt that the loss of friends is one of the heaviest prices to pay for gaining the new world. On the other hand, emigrating is also an opportunity to do a serious spring clean amongst friends. Living away forces you to realise who your true friends are. It results in you having a clearer picture of how you can be a true friend in spite the physical distance. The much-abused term of spending "quality time" together gets a new meaning, a bit like the thirsty man in the desert who is offered only half a glass of water. But the water is ice cold and life giving. Not a drop must be spilled. The contact will intensify and can bring useful learning into other areas of our lives.

New friends

We can experience how immigration almost automatically makes us more open towards new friendships. The new environment increases our willingness to engage with others and every encounter has the seeds of learning and personal development. This positive development can co-exist with the looming paranoia previously discussed, and is to all intents and purposes the paranoia's only real antidote. However, many immigrants complain about their inability to form the same level of profound friendships abroad as they could at home. They never feel they really become 'part of the gang' and seem only to achieve status as permanent observers.

You cannot share a laugh in any genuine way about silly television programs from 20 years ago, public figures or children's sayings with your new world friends. The pool of shared history is simply not there. It is nobody's fault and is probably partly due to language, partly due to lack of common frame of reference and the battle of values as discussed above. It *is* a loss.

Partner

The fresh openness of the newcomer of course also appeals to the opposite sex. Relationships of intimate nature can be started in ways that you in old world would not have thought possible. Your daringness, pace and luck may be very different from that which you have been used to back home. A strong sense of "nothing to lose" and your newly acquired status of being "a rare bird" definitely play a part in this new, or at least enhanced, adventurousness.

Not infrequently long term partners are found under these circumstances and such relationships give an excellent opportunity to "pick and mix" from different cultures. In spite of the joys of mutual eclecticism, mixed partnerships can nevertheless also be a combustible interaction (see Battle of values). Entrenched ideas that so far have been seen as irrefutable truths will be challenged, and this can cause much disharmony. But it is on the whole a very healthy process. It just takes shiploads of flexibility and tolerance.

Just as you are not personally responsible for the ills of your own native country, neither is he or she responsible for the host country's problems. It is tempting to vent your anger and frustration on the closest representative for the offending country when things are not going your way. This puts an undue strain on relationships. Personal experience tells me this.

Chapter V

Visits

It takes a very special friend to
forgive you your successes."
Oscar Wilde

Returning home for visits

There is something indescribable about the first return to the old world after a substantial amount of time (months or years) away. It feels like a pilgrimage to a place for which you have longed for a life time. A creeping feeling of euphoria starting in the lower abdomen spreading all over may actually prevent you from doing any serious work for a long time before you leave the new world. The excitement of contemplating all the people you want to see, places you want to revisit and old world-situations you want to re-experience is intoxicating. It is in fact so intoxicating, that it can become addictive – this may be an important factor in keeping you from returning to the old world for good.

Already, weeks before a planned return, you start feel slightly lightheaded from sheer anticipation. A vague image may take shape in your mind, that of a grand reception in the airport by huge numbers of well wishers, not unlike the triumphant reception enjoyed by victorious Roman soldiers returning to Rome. In your eyes, you will receive a well earned pat on the back from the people you grew up with; you, who have conquered a scary, new world all on your own, deserve the most extraordinary recognition from your kinsmen.

Unfortunately few airport reception of the above-mentioned splendor has been known to befall the returning emigrant. However, unfair as it may appear, the 'conquest of the new world' is usually more the

147

view of the returning emigrant than it is that of those whom he had left behind.

Status has changed

Having said that, your status in the eyes of the people of the old world will have changed forever by the simple fact of you having been able to survive abroad. The old world people may not openly admit it, but their view of you has changed forever. Nobody can deny that status means something to all of us. We are, after all, gregarious animals that have an innate drive to better our standing in the group. This change in status is also reflected by most future employers who certainly in the majority of cases do recognise this specific asset on your CV. The same curiously goes for future (and current) partners who will also realise that you have just proven something significant by surviving in a different culture - perhaps a superior ability to survive in a Darwinistic sense. And they are right.

All your social survival skills have been challenged to a degree that would never have occurred back home. You having survived is ample evidence that your adaptability is attractive both professionally and erotically. Adaptability is the essential cornerstone in what it takes to be a successful human being. It may very well be that comforting knowledge, even if unconscious, that you have moved on in the fast lane is what lies beneath the excitement of returning home.

Why did they not come?

The reason for the absence of splendour of the reception in the airport from anybody, apart from the immediate family and friends, is also partly down to a fear of acknowledging that you have changed for the stronger. This statement may not make straightforward sense. But a well-known phenomenon in group psychology is that when someone leaves for another place, job or group, this place inevitably becomes a better, more exciting place in the imagination of those left behind.

That may in reality not be the case at all. For all they know, you could have gone abroad and struggled hard to survive, but still people in the old world would have a tendency in their minds to glamorise your – to them – unknown life in a foreign land. This inclination has of course been exploited numerous times by both 'big' and 'small' people in order to make the most of their achievements on their return. All, from failed explorers to mediocre businessmen and academics, have attempted to fool the old world people with tall stories of various levels of success.

Tell the truth

The father of good friend tried this little trick more than 40 years ago. It came back to haunt him later in a very unexpected way. As a young medical student, he was examined by a professor and an external examiner for his gynecology exam. The young man was very keen on the subject and he had already at this early stage decided to make this specialty his future career. The examination went smoothly until the old professor asked the student how big an ovarian cyst could become. The flustered student waffled a bit before he burst out: "25 litres."

The two examiners look knowingly at each other and smiled forbearingly – they had never heard about cysts growing beyond 5 litres. Thinking on his feet, the young man quickly replied that during a stay in Germany he had visited the anatomical museum in the University of Magdeburg that had a specimen of an ovary containing a cyst in excess of 25 liters. They examiners were deeply impressed and rewarded the dedicated student with the top mark.

15 years later the young man had turned into a distinguished consultant gynecologist and the old professor to a retired professor. On his way back to Denmark from a holiday in Italy the old professor persuaded his wife to drop by Magdeburg as they were going through Germany anyway. Once in the streets of Magdeburg he stopped the car and asked in his best schoolboy German a surprised by-passer for directions to the University.

"Aber hier gibt's überhaupt keine Universitat..." ("there is no university here at all..."), was the surprised German's answer.

Incensed, the old man returned to Denmark and phoned up my friend's father in a fury. He threatened him with all kinds of reprisals for his youthful fraud. The young consultant must somehow have been able to ride out the storm because he is to this day in a senior position in a Copenhagen hospital, and, I presume, a little more suspicious of fantastical claims made by ambitious students.

This imaginative approach cannot be recommended, especially, not in a time of electronic communication where information can be verified with greater ease than in the time of Columbus! Your personal integrity is an asset that under no circumstances must be blemished.

Green grass

After having left a job in a psychotherapy hospital in London, I was told years later by old colleagues that people in the psychotherapy group in which I had worked thought that I had either gone back to my home country to marry an attractive long lost, Danish beauty queen, or been appointed professor at another London hospital. In fact, I was an unemployed, junior doctor still living with his English girlfriend… whom I did not tell that I quite liked my ex-patients' ideas.

It is not difficult to understand that envy caused by these kinds of fantasies can dampen other people's enthusiasm for hearing about your experiences in the new world.

Envy works both ways
Envy nevertheless does work both ways. Visiting old friends, it can appear to you that their lives seem so more comfortable, stable and secure than your own. They may have settled down in a nice old world area amidst all your old friends and their families. They may even at this stage have a family of their own. They may be having a barbeque for you on a lovely summer's evening with their children peacefully running around playing in the mild breeze. During such moments, restless souls can find it tough to keep soppy sentiments at bay.

If we manage to steer clear of the clammy grip of sentimentality and repetitive stories from the olden days during our meetings with old friends, they can give us a rare sense of permanence in an ever faster spinning world, a sense that although some bridges behind us have collapsed, some will have survived or even been strengthened. It is worth remembering that all bridges behind you, collapsed or still standing, will provide you with rich material to build new ones ahead of you.

Nevertheless, almost immediately after having returned to the old world, an air of sanity descends. People do what people are supposed to do; it can be as mundane as riding their bicycles, selling things in the street or going through a red light. Whatever the norm is in your old world, people do it. Home-comings awaken the same emotions that go through the mind and body of a lost child being reunited with its mother, a rediscovery of a solid point of reference in an otherwise nomadic existence. A languishing and starving corner of your soul jubilantly replenishes itself. Your mind has been struggling to get used to all the changes abroad and suddenly, things fall back into place. More or less, at least. Ten years on, this pervasive emotion still strikes me when I return to my native Denmark. It is as reassuring as a dummy in the mouth of an anxious toddler.

Emotions allowed
On a more practical level it is damn good to see mum, dad, friends and familiar circumstances again – a bit like jumping straight back into a picture you had fallen out of some time ago. You are back in a context that understands your jokes without explanations, where you can come up with remarks about the past that will be picked up readily by those around you, and where language is no longer a problem, either linguistically or culturally. Suddenly it is allowed to be much more emotional with both friends and family than was usually the case when you lived at home. Nobody turns their noses up at you for hugging your friends and kissing your friends of the opposite sex – which for me, coming from a cold, northern European country, is not the usual state of affairs. The intensity experienced in the greetings can translate into better relationships.

Those normally insignificant exchanges at the check-out point make themselves significant by the very fact of being even more insignificant than under the circumstances to which you have become accustomed; for once your accent did not tell on you. The cashier did not look at you for that second longer because you did not quite sound as the indigenous people. You call up a restaurant to make a reservation and you no longer have to spell your name because around there it is common.

Not that these small things really bother you in the new world, but it is nice to be conventionally inconspicuous just every now and then – a state of affairs that is rarely possible in the new world because of your differentness; your accent, your funny name and perhaps even your looks. You can breathe a sigh of relief.

You can see!

Exploring your own country, its countryside, its history and its people now takes an unprecedented place in your life. You can find yourself gravitating to places that represent stability – the stability you have lost in your new life. But it is also as if the immigration process has given your back your eyesight. The very eyesight that years of habituation had stolen away before you left. A humdrum trip to the local villages that would have bored you to tears in the past, gives the returning immigrant an opportunity to dive into his people's background, where he came from and appraise what he has become. Reading the history of your people, finding out about your family history and meeting family members become critically important. This archeology into your own past is a way of stocking up on ammunition ready to return to the onslaught on your embattled identity by the new world hordes. You are reminding yourself about your background and thereby cementing your distinctiveness to weather foreign storms.

The common experience of the adult returning to his childhood playground and finding that it has now shrunk into a diminutive caricature of its former self is, for the visiting immigrant, even more noticeable. Old world distances seem shorter, buildings smaller and people less threatening, all testimony to the distance covered by you while you have been away. Homeland exploration may also serve exactly that purpose, giving you a clearer picture of how far you have come - not unlike looking up old friends from your old world life: "Where am I now... where was I when I left... could I have been there now if I had stayed?" Background-exploring helps by giving clues to some of these fundamental questions.

Immigrants having left because they hated their role in the old world society may return just to gather evidence that things have not changed since they left. This regularly leads to highly biased information collection. But off they go to continue their new world life with fewer regrets, while their regrets about the old world life have become more entrenched.

The past

Life is inevitably hard on the inexperienced emigrant, but early returns to the old world also serve to remind him that the misery is not a permanent state of affairs. The spell can be broken - the rawness that can be so painful early on during the emigration process can be treated with a good dose of the old world. But it would be a fallacy to believe that two parallel universes can be created. They cannot, and a choice must be made about which universe you want to inhabit. The past is for understanding, not for living in.

It is tough to be a star

The returns are almost unavoidably lived in an explosion of hectic activity. The phone is ringing; people have heard you are back, wanting to see you. There may be a touch bitterness that they were told about your return by others and not by you. For this reason, and for the better reason that you want to see them, you try to fit them into an already overbooked diary. "Could we meet for breakfast?" is your latest attempt to survive the fervour. Everyone must be squeezed into the heavy schedule. It is tough to be a star.

It can sometimes feel that you are ticking off people on a list instead of enjoying sorely missed company. It can leave you with a twinge of bad conscience which is not made better by friends' comments such as:

"Already... but we will see you again before you go... won't we?"

Making the cut
The experienced immigrant will, after a couple of visits to the old world, cut the 'ticking' list to a bare minimum. On certain shorter trips with specific goals (e.g. birthdays, funerals, meetings) you may have to sneak into your own country "incognito" simply to avoid offending friends and family members that would find it odd that you had come back without visiting them. Some harsh choices must be made, and little by little a new A-list of the selected few emerges. The selected few may not be the ones you would have predicted prior to leaving the old world.

Weeding out friends is not a pleasant process, but a necessary one, that can add to your personal understanding of what you value in others.

Please come back
It is not uncommon that friends genuinely missing you will attempt to lure you back to the old world during your rushed visits. Both carrot and stick is used by old friends behaving not unlike scorned lovers.

"Oh, please come back... think of all the people that you would be able to see every day, the old world specialties (ranging from Christmas traditional food to old world films) you would be able to have if only you came back."

"What are you still doing in the new world? Come back now or you will die as a lonely oddball tucked away in some foreign country without really being close to anybody."

Variations on the theme exist but the gist is clear. These people want you back. Whether it is for your or their benefit is less clear. You must realize that while the carrot method can be acceptable in moderate doses, the stick approach is by definition wrong. Those who wield a stick can under no circumstances know enough about your new world life to be able to make a cogent judgment. They know about life in the old world and may have their own reasons for berating you for your infidelity. Could it be that they would have liked to have done what you did but lacked the courage? Could it be that life in the old world is not so brilliant and that they would be pretty hard pushed to accept that life could be livable elsewhere? Could it be that they are so narrow-minded that they cannot imagine a life outside their own little, blinkered comfort zone? And lastly, could they be right?

These are all possibilities that you need to consider.

Weighed and measured

It cannot be denied that returning home has an air of assessment-time hanging over it. You may, in the weeks leading up to the visit, suddenly feel like loosing a few pounds, dyeing your hair to cover the grey patches or buying some new clothes. The thought of how people will perceive you back home after all this time will cross most immigrants' minds. "Will they notice that I have changed, will they accept me"?

This sense of a pending exam is an important contributor to the 'butterflies in the stomach' before returning. This nervousness may contribute to the difficulties in striking the right balance between over- and underplaying your hand in conversation with old friends and relatives back in the old world. You have a clear urge to tell your story – sometimes it appears that you have not really savoured what you have experienced properly until you have told someone about it. You can find yourself anxiously vacillating between wanting to tell them how much you have achieved and all the problems you have encountered, and how much you have missed them while you were away. Too many success stories can drive a wedge between old friends and you can subsequently feel obliged to elaborate more on the negative aspects of immigrant-life. Generally, it is a better idea to wait to be asked to explain about your new world life than to overload the audience with information uninvited. Holding back a little will give you a clearer impression about how much they really want to know. It is a fine line. You always have to be on the look out for signs of envy even in old friends and relatives (see later). Envy is a complex human emotion that can toxify relationships of long standing.

Gore Vidal admitted that whenever a friend succeeded, a little something in him died.

Emotional obstruction

It can leave you with a feeling of emotional obstruction. The best thing to do is to let them out in small doses while always remaining vigilant to others' reaction. But on the other hand do not sacrifice your precious time at home trying to be pardoned. Some people can only take minimal doses, while others can deal with considerably more – largely depending on how much at ease they are with their own lives.

It is advisable to be guided by how you feel, and choose to talk about the subjects that you feel comfortable with. Do not become overwhelmed by the expectations of others. A policy of incremental sincerity usually stands both you and your friends and relatives in good stead despite initial trepidations.

A feast

Safely back in the old world you may feel a certain impulse to go up to strangers in the street that speak your language in sheer delight of hearing your mother tongue again. Someone who has not heard or spoken his or her own language for a long time can feel like veritably deprived. Getting the chance to use your language again is like rediscovering a dear old friend who has been brutally tucked away for a long time in a dusty cupboard. Like most people who have been stuffed away in cramped places without exercise, the joints are initially stiff and have lost confidence in their ability to move effortlessly.

Old expressions you have not heard for years will explode in your ears like fireworks. With surprising speed the stooped man from the cupboard learns to carry himself with pride. It is a feast, a feast on words.

Smells that you have not experienced for years can catapult you back in time more forcefully than any other sensory modality is able to. A whiff of the seemingly innocuous smells of old world food, earth, sea or even people can conjure up the most amazingly vivid images of situations that you had believed to be long forgotten. Such a free tour of your past can be deeply moving.

An ill-fitting shoe

There is however often a nagging feeling that all is not right. You have during your new world stay been feeling like a foot in an ill-fitting shoe. Now you have returned to realize that the shoe you left behind in the old world no longer fits either. The period you have been away has changed both you and the old world. People you used to see on a daily basis may suddenly look older, new words have crept into the language and television programmes have been replaced by new ones. All of this has occurred without your consent.

Status quo is, as previously mentioned, not compatible with the human condition but very compatible with our memories. Strangely enough, status quo is a fallacy even in seemingly the most stagnant of contexts. We are always striving in a direction. The old world may appear unchanged, but it is no longer the same place that you left. Even after a relative short period away. For better and for worse.

Relationships do not escape the passing time. Even after shorter periods of no face-to-face contact, from weeks to months, it is not uncommon to feel that a certain distance has come between you and the most intimate relationships in the old world. The reason for this distance is a combination of new things having happened in both parties' lives, but for all, an acute sense that protection against the unknown is needed. Both parties feel out of touch with the other person, unsure of what the other person has experienced in the intervening period and what is expected.

Relationships

Let us look in greater detail at the relationship with old world people. Could anything have happened to threaten those well grounded relationships? Does he/she still see me with the same eyes as before?

Despite the fact that the answers to these questions in all honesty usually are "Yes" and "No" respectively, the most by far of these problems can be overcome with a bit of time and patience from both sides. They may see you as a threat to their stable life in old world. You may see them as a temptation to abandon your foreign dreams and head home for easier life. Your best friend's wife may think that you are about to encourage her meek husband to join you "out there" and leave her in the old world with the kids. You may feel that these people are stuck in exactly the same rut as when you left long time ago. At first glance nothing seems to have changed in their lives.

It cannot be denied that an important part of visiting home is to take stock of how far you have come since you left a situation not dissimilar to theirs. It is like looking over your shoulder from a safe distance. This process invariably invites comparison between what you had and what you have.

Learned helplessness
Your friends may by now remind you of the famous psychologist Seligman's rat experiments in the 60s; an electric current was led through part of the metal floor of their cages. Some animals would immediately seek out the un-electrified part of the cage. Others would follow their example as the electric current was turned up. But surprisingly, a group of animals would not budge regardless of how strong the current was. They would curl up in the same place and patiently wait to be electrocuted. Seligman called this phenomenon "learned helplessness". You may be seeing your friends in this light because it is the truth, or more commonly, because you need to strengthen your own resolve to stick it out in the new world.

The human ability to build bridges is nevertheless quite extraordinary, especially when we accept a degree of uncertainty in our relationships and accept that things will never be exactly as they were before. The alternative is an unbearable level of control-freakery and ultimately, isolation.

A young female friend of mine described how painful it was that her beloved father seemed less interested in her life in an American university than when she lived back in Denmark. She believed that she, by being away, had created a new room in the house of her soul that even her father could not visit. During visits to America she felt he could do nothing more than stand in the doorway of her new room and look around in timid amazement. He was unable to participate in her new life in the way he used to while she was living in Copenhagen. She also talked about her old world friends' seeming lack of interest in her life abroad. She put it down to a degree of envy but also to the simple inability to imagine what her life could possibly be like so many thousands of kilometers away. She had on a couple of occasions on her visits to Copenhagen attempted to show photos to her old world people, but had rarely got further than the first few pictures before their interest ebbed away.

She refused to take it personally, but recognized the pain of being unable to share everything with people who used to know most things about her. Sensibly she concluded that she still had most of the things she had always had with the old world people, but that she, by adding a new room to "her house" had simply expanded her capacity. She was now able to invite other people into her extension – people that previously she would have missed out on. The main part of her house remains occupied by old world people, at least for the time being.

Euphoria

It is the strangest things that a visit to the Old world can cause a peculiar sense of euphoria; simply by walking down a familiar street, or being in your childhood bedroom, or stuffing yourself with local treats that are unavailable in the new world. It is paradoxically a sure sign of enlarged horizon that one is now able to experience small, apparently unimportant things, with such intensity. The intensity serves mainly two purposes – to remind you where you came from and where you have come to. That leaves you with a clearer picture of the distance between these two points.

Taking a bus that you used to take to school, walking into a shop where you did the shopping with your mother and even meeting long lost friends, bring back so many memories. Perhaps most importantly memories not about situations, but about you – the way you were – when you were last in that situation. It can be a very powerful deja-vu occurrence. It may be a sensation of happiness or despair that grabs you when you walk in the streets of your childhood town, but memory is far from a source of exact information, rather a link to what you felt at the time.

When it happens is not possible to say. Peculiarly, things can, as mentioned before, appear to have shrunk while you have been away. Houses seem less imposing, distances shorter, people less intimidating and problems more manageable. Perhaps the greatest gift of long term travelling is the unperceived process of rearranging things on the inner shelves of importance. This fundamental rearrangement is caused by a new macrocosmic perception of the world. The comforting microcosmic view, where the ups and downs of the local football team tended to dictate your moods, are lost forever. Regional, old world accents that used to have a bearing on your attitude to others have paled into appropriate insignificance.

Your perspective has changed forever and cannot willfully be restored to what it was before. You have given yourself a chance to see things from different angles and thereby get a better sense of the real proportions of life.

Ambiguity

You will towards the end of your stay in the old world feel a certain degree of ambiguity about returning to the new world. You have been very excited about seeing your old friends and family and are now about to return to the new world with its eternal lack of genuine homeliness. The original wounds incurred from leaving the old world in the first place are ripped open all over again. The reasons why you originally left may still be attracting you to go abroad combined with the fact that you have built up a life in the new world. On the other hand you enjoyed yourself on the holiday in the old world, seeing friends, relaxing and taking things in so intensely. But it does not give you a realistic picture of how life is really lived in the old world. A holiday trip may easily give you a pleasant but slightly rosy picture of how things are back home. This is not a good basis on which to make a decision about returning for good.

It is not unheard of for people to decide to stay and not return to the new world after a holiday in the old world. This can lead to bitter disappointments, and the decision is better taken at a less emotional time, e.g. after having spent more time in either of the two worlds.

Goodbyes

The goodbyes are never easy. It can be almost physically painful to have to separate yourself from loved-ones. The nineteen century poet Tennyson's statement that "to have lost and loved, is better than not to have loved at all" can seem pretty far-fetched in these situations. Attachment hurts.

It can be tempting to sneak away unseen just to avoid the finality of the goodbye. Like most problems in life brushing problems under the carpet is not to be recommended. Goodbyes have to be faced up to in order to be able to say a proper hello in the future. Be consoled by Marcel Proust's words, that at the moment of departure, it is always the one who truly loves, who cannot find his words. Face the pain of acknowledging your parting paths and feel better for it. Saying goodbye reminds you that nothing is forever and can enhance appreciation of situations and people.

Even after a shorter period of time away a visit to the old world will make you notice changes in yourself. Maybe this is the key reason for the return. It is if there is a need to touch base to realise the enormity of what has been achieved while away. You will become aware of newfound courage to say things that you would have left unsaid in the past.

Coming back to your new world home, however makeshift it may be, can be a blissful experience. This is a sure sign that something has changed inside. You will now be better at standing your ground because you have gained one of the greatest insights that immigrant life can give you; that a happy life can be lived elsewhere.

Visits from home
People visiting from the old world are always a big occasion; inspectors sent out to gaze on how you are coping. You are not forgotten. You will cut your hair, mow your lawn, paint your house – well aware of the

importance of this state visit on your position back in the old world, as well your sense of well-being. This is your chance to prove that your decision to get up and leave was right.

Such a visit is always envisaged with heightened emotions. It is a rare treat to be allowed to rekindle old friendships under distant skies. But will they like your new world life at all? Will they approve? Will they see you as you would like to be seen?

Often these questions are not all prominent in the visitors' minds as they are in yours. They feel insecure about both practical and social issues in the new country and can be quite dependent on your expert guidance. "How much is this amount of monopoly money in real money? Do they have stamps in this country? What do those road signs mean? How long will it take me to get to X-town?" Some of their insecurities may make you chuckle secretly and remind you about your own first period of time in the new world. Being a host for old world visitors means something other than what you have become accustomed to. You may even start to feel responsible for the new world weather during the visit.

You used to be able to just walk down the road to see these people but suddenly a meeting like this has taken on a whole new meaning. So many things need to be cramped into a short encounter. You will often over-plan and fill up the agenda with numerous visits and activities to make sure that they see it all. Every second counts. During a short visit, you want to have your old friends back, show the new world, show them what you have done and at the same time convince them that you are still the same deep down and pose no threat to the life they have chosen. It is hard to do in such a short span of time!

Things have changed

Initially, the expectations, the separation and the new territory (for the guests) can make it appear difficult to establish your former intimacy. Worries about how you will get on and whether the spark between you is still there will always be present to some degree... have things changed since you saw them the last time?

The answer to that question is, yes, absolutely, things have changed. But the fact that your lives are so very different now compared to then does not inevitably mean that you have drifted apart irreparably. Far from it. A short reunion with representatives from the old world can have all the intensity and fire that many of our every day life contacts lack, because we take them for granted.

At the beginning it is usually a good approach to engage in something fairly neutral like showing the visitors the sights of the new world while you hastily attempt to acclimatize to each other and make up for lost time. Your mutual history is also a safe bet to break the ice: "Do you remember when Janice was sick in your lab..." etc.

It is not unusual, because of the different context of your meeting in the new world, that new and hitherto unexplored avenues open up between you; suddenly you can touch on subjects that in the humdrum of old world life would have not have been discussed. Your relationship has been granted yet another facet thanks to unfamiliarity of the context.

It can be extremely bizarre to observe your visiting old world friends or relatives communicate with your new world friends; it appears as an unforeseen merger in your mind of worlds that until that moment have appeared separated by light years. Your new world as well as old world friends will often, after such a meeting, see you in a quite a new light – both groups feeling a bit puzzled and curious about the life you have elsewhere. A feeling of pride that you have contributed to the novel interconnectedness of your worlds is not uncommon, and can be the seed of much longed-for peace of mind.

Moving on
Avoid lingering on the issues that made you leave the old world, as an apprehensive visitor could easily misconstrue this as condescending aggression. These issues are often at the forefront of your mind – sometimes distorted out of proportion – in order to help you getting through the difficult time of settling in the new world. Seeing an old friend from back home can remind you about the old world difficulties that you used to be able to discuss passionately together. But now the balance has tipped. You took the opportunity and left, while he is still having to put up with them. It is admittedly tempting to go over the old world irritants once again to bolster up your own courage to stay on in the new world, but if you choose to do it at all, go easy on the dosage and monitor reactions carefully.

Under normal circumstances you get back into the swing of the things with each other relatively quickly. Only exceptions are if one of the parties has a chip on his or her shoulder for reasons that usually go way back, and may not even be related to you personally. Rest assured that making the effort to come all that way to see you is sufficient evidence that these people really care about you.

Walking down a new world street with an old world friend speaking your old world language can make you feel invincible. The feeling of being detached from the everyday humdrum of the new world life can induce a surge of confidence that is difficult to match. You are happy that they came.

You will however often be struck by your visitors' perception of your adopted country. Even fairly sophisticated people's view of the country may be based on some ill-informed clichés they have picked up over the years (see stereotypes). They need to be put right in a diplomatic way. Exasperation can be avoided by thinking about what your impression of the new world was when you first arrived. The best way of nailing myths – as you have learned - is to actually be there and investigate matters for yourself. Your visitors have just shown great commitment to that, and to you, by coming all the way to the new world.

Demanding business
Catching up with friends or relatives from the old world can be a highly demanding business that can leave you utterly exhausted at the end of an even short stay. However, in my experience it is well worth it. After a while in the new world it is refreshing to communicate with someone from your own culture with a similar frame of reference to your own. They will intuitively pick up on new world things that you find either intriguing or annoying because of relatively similar basic values laid down long ago in both of you. Sometimes during your new world life it can feel as if you are going crazy because some of your fundamental beliefs seemed to be held by you only. Chances are that visitors from the old world will reconfirm your sanity.

You will often, from these encounters with the old world, both visits from and to the old world, bring along with you a mental "doggy-bag" of all the things that was said and done. Long after the visit is over you will be able to take out the goodies from this bag and smile quietly to yourself. It can make you feel so tremendously rich.

Visits from home not only establish that links to the old world have not been severed, but we also get a feeling for how our lives could have been had we continued down the original road back home. It is obviously not a very precise picture of how things would have turned out, but visitors from the old world nevertheless make us consider the big "if I had stayed…"question. It makes you realize how different your life is now and what you miss from home, but fortunately also what you have achieved by venturing outside of your own neck of the woods. After such visits the answer to this all-important question can become clearer in your mind - at least momentarily.

Chapter VI

Returning home for good

"Travelling is the ruin of all happiness! There is no looking at a building here after seeing Italy."

Fanny Burney

Returning home

Clive James, an Australian immigrant who has lived in the UK for decades wrote: "Pulsing like a beacon through the days and nights, the birthplace of the fortunate sends out its invisible waves of recollection. It always has and it always will, until even the last of us come home."

For many people – if not for all - who have lived abroad for many years the dream about returning home one day stays intact. Some may act on this dream, some may not. What divides these two groups is a mixture of personality, experiences dating back both from the old and the new world, residual drive, physical health and above all, the ability to integrate. The returners probably consist of the sub-group of immigrants that has integrated the least well, and, strangely enough, also the sub-group that has integrated with the most ease. The first group return for the obvious reason that they cannot find any joy in the new world, and the latter because they believe that they can effortlessly re-integrate back into the old world.

The process of re-integration is however by no means any less complicated than integrating, though the experienced gained first time round is valuable. Cain's readmission back into Paradise was never going to be easy!

Same, same but different

Sometimes personal or work conditions dictate a speedy return, but the decision to return home for good is usually taken after long considerations and considerable dithering. Driven by an urge to reduce the pace and peacefully return for quiet reflection after years of hectic activity spurs on many immigrants to take the plunge. The inner scale-balance is once again brought out to be studied intensely. What counts for and what counts against? The same fear as when you originally left may re-emerge; "Can I make it? Will I be accepted? How will people see me?" The fear rarely reaches quite the same fever pitch as before the first emigration, but the uncertainty is definitely there once again. Clint Eastwood has suggested that if you ever want a guarantee, you should buy a toaster.

Old demons

Other fears creep in; fear of facing again some of demons left behind those many years ago; a long lost friendship or relationship, the way other people saw you then, and a by now unfamiliar sense of being just an ordinary old world person living in the old world. But this is not a time for emotional reasoning. There must be rational reasons for the return, elderly parents, or the children's school, or friends, or other weighty reasons for believing that life would in some important way be richer back home. Jotting these reasons down on paper increases the chance of getting a clearer picture in your mind about what is really important and what is not. It also reduces the risk of you feeling miserable on your eventual return. There will of course still be difficult times ahead but the piece of paper outlining why it was you wanted to return to the old world after all these years will come in handy in pressurised situations after returning. No matter which decision is reached there will be prices to pay, but equally prizes to win.

Overselling the old world

Convincing a potential new world partner to join you in your native country is not always straightforward. Many strategies will be needed to coax them into leaving their world and following you into the unknown. Your portrayal of your old world can be slightly coloured, partly by your desire to bring back your trophy partner, partly because of a genuine recall bias that has left you an over-positive memory of your past (see chapter IV). You are, in other words, overselling your old world. It is a very dangerous policy and the 'trophy' may kick up a hell of a fuss when it realises the reality of things. It feels like a double whammy when you make the same realisation. You will be the target of blame and blows; "It is all your fault".

It puts a strain on the relationship that can only be pre-empted by the greatest degree of honesty and openness from an early stage.

To stay is also to live

A substantial number of immigrants struggle to settle down after returning home for good. There is little doubt that settling down is not helped by the fact that immigrants as a group are already predisposed to a tendency to believe the grass is greener on the other side. They may have taken to heart the fairytale writer Hans Christian Andersen's words that "to travel is to live" without realising that while travelling is definitely associated with living, staying can be too.

The reasons why emigrants originally left their old country and culture have often dwindled into insignificance over the years of struggling with the challenges of the new world. As it is customary for the human mind – and I presume a sign of good mental health – we tend to view our past through rose-tinted spectacles. The further away into the past the thicker the spectacles become! Only the positive experiences are honoured with any space in our memories. This kind of selective recall may keep us sane while we are gone, but it does not always serve the purpose of giving us an accurate picture of what we can expect on our return. The original reasons for leaving may suddenly emerge to hit the returner right on the chin on his eventual arrival back home. You can feel trapped in a claustrophobic spider's web of past and present merging, with nowhere left to run. This human interconnectedness can rarely be escaped, and the illusion of being free is hence so tragically violated.

"Oh no, are they still talking about those same, dreary, insular topics here... I can't believe that this arrogance still is the prevailing attitude back here", etc., etc.

Simultaneously, there is an unique opportunity to try to reconcile yourself with the demons of the past, having the obvious benefit of the more experienced man's vantage point. The original problems may be the same - you are not.

Society has changed

The speed with which societies change is nevertheless incredible – especially when one is removed from them. Even after a few years away a culture may have changed almost beyond recognition. It is as if an invisible broom has swept away everything you knew. Returning is certainly not the same as going back to the past you once knew. The past cannot be reconstructed. Not long ago some New Zealanders would still get moist eyes when talking about "going home", meaning returning to their forefathers' native Britain of 100 years ago. Most of the families I met during my stay in New Zealand in the 80s had by then been in the South Pacific for three or four generations. This kind of misguided sense of belonging is bound to lead to unrealistic expectations. But maybe the images of old England with cricket pitches, chocolate box villages and steam trains served the purpose of always providing a dreamy alternative when the harshness of pioneering life became too much. But now, as life for New Zealanders has become more comfortable over the years, there has been a decline in open displays of allegiance to the British and their Queen.

A change for the better
Deep down in most immigrants rests a secret desire for things not to change at home; this one, sacred place in the whole world should remain untouched by the relentlessness of never-ending change. All this is in sharp contrast to the life lived abroad. The immigrant would for years have used the romanticised, mental image of the old world as a buffer against uncertainties and injustice encountered in the new world. He had been holding on to this island of stability in an ocean of seismic change, a mental bank account of glossy pictures to be drawn upon in times of trouble. Unlike other accounts, the assets here become stronger and more entrenched with every withdrawal.

Change is not necessarily for the worse. The re-integrator realizes fast that the sun soaked meadows of yester-year is now a new housing estate with high levels of youth crime and granny's old cottage has been turned into a MacDonald's serving the passing motorway. In spite of nostalgia for the meadows, the successful re-integrator also realises that this housing estate for the underprivileged is far better than the

175

accommodation the same group of people would have lived in when he left. Similarly, he does sometimes get hungry while driving on the motorway. In other words, development is not always for the worse just because you have not been there to witness it. It is essential not to condemn mindlessly the custodians of the old world for not having looked after the crown jewels while you were away. If you do, your relationship to the custodians could rapidly turn sour.

Images, thoughts, behaviours and attitudes that have served us well do not die easily.

An opponent to change

But in this case they will have to! Or if not die, at least step discreetly into the background. It is a certain road to bitterness and isolation if the returner does not come to terms with the discrepancy between his inner image of the old world and the real, present-day one. It is not unusual that the worldly returner paradoxically becomes the most ardent opponent of even the smallest change, such as new door knobs in the apartment building, or moving the furniture around. This is not the kind of behaviour that inspires great adoration in others who may quickly start to get annoyed with the returner. This in turn could start a negative circle of unconstructive events counterproductive to re-integration. The beloved old world can soon start to look like an unfriendly and hostile place – far removed from the nurtured image that you had brought with you for all the years abroad. No degree in psychology is needed to understand that great gaps between the imagined world and the real one are a highway to frustration and low mood.

The fact of societal fluidity must permeate the skull, even the thickest. It may help to realise that the inner image you had of the old world probably never existed quite the way you remembered it anyway.

Between two stools

Another potential problem for the re-integrator is the sense of having placed yourself linguistically between two stools. Your speak the new language to a good level and may actually find it difficult to find the correct – especially professional - terms in your native language after having worked abroad for a number of years. But you still cannot master it to perfection. Your old world language is rusty and needs brushing up. This process can be highly wearisome. You will find yourself struggling to find simple expressions in your own mother tongue, desperately wanting to replace them with new world words to which you have become so accustomed. Also, you have not been exposed to years of linguistic development in your homeland and the old world people may mock you for your antiquated and clumsy way of expressing yourself. It can be very annoying, especially if for years you have harboured a dream of returning to your own culture and cutting them all down to size with a single swing of your eloquent tongue to compensate for all the times the same tongue has let you down in the new world. Please note however that old world people's mockery often contains a subtle undertone of admiration for what you have done.

Some short-term immigrants can take pride in the fact of being "alien" – however slight its manifestation may be. They overdo their accents and their foreign ways in their contact with old world people. Few societies deal leniently with 'fake' re-integrators and their accents seem to fade within a fortnight.

Pieces fall in to place

The degree of problems you have with your childhood language is clearly linked to length of stay, to whether you had a native language partner and to the degree of exposure to your own language you experienced while away. In some ways returning home for good is not dissimilar to having got up from one dinner table at a party and moved on to the next table. On your return to the original table you cannot expect to pick up the conversation right away.

The strategy to overcome these problems is very similar to when you arrived in the new world; place yourself in situations that give opportunities to listen, and speak the language that once was your only means of communicating. Read the newspapers, travel your old world, speak to others (especially younger people) to get a feeling for the changes that have taken place in your absence. You will find that things fall into place like pieces in a jigsaw puzzle that has been thrown up in the air and stayed there for the time were away. As a result of your trained vigilance you will end up with quite a few more pieces than when you left. That is not such a bad deal – though it can complicate the process of putting it back together again!

I recently attended a dinner party in my native country and, as the host's job is to understand the mind of criminals, we naturally discussed violence and serial murders. The name of P.T. came up and I innocently asked who he was. The host was absolutely dumbfounded. How could a man of my stature not know?

Well, for the simple reason that I was not in this country at the time P.T. committed his murders. The useful old excuse about not knowing something because you are a poor foreigner does not apply as easily in this context (see chapter IV). Your time of amnesty has come to an abrupt end. Your language, looks and behaviour are too local for others to be led to believe that you need special help. A quiet remark to remind them about your long absence is probably the best way forward.

A circle is closed
Psychologically, returning home is also a real challenge. The reality is usually nothing like the image of the lost paradise created by the frustrations experienced in the new world. Unsought, the return to the old world closes a circle which before was open ended, and from which you benefited from for years. When you were in the new world, you were seen as exciting and different as a result of being foreign. When you visited the old world you were the brave dare-devil who had had the courage to break away from the beaten track and do something different.

A brick in no one's wall. All in all it provided you with a greatly enhanced sense of being special everywhere you went. It can be highly addictive, an enticing kick for any narcissist! That circle of grandeur is effectively closed the moment you return for good. You are bricked up in your own house. To hit the world of anonymity so suddenly is 'cold turkey' with longlasting withdrawal symptoms. This is perhaps why many returned emigrants never talk about returning home to spend the rest of their lives there but rather about "taking each day as it comes, and never ruling out going back travelling." It is too painful to have let go of the idea of "the other life" where things are different and everyday life does not exist. A whole industry has been build on the notion of "the other life" because most people need that dream to get through the daily grind; the dream of hotels, travel agents, travel books on Provence, Tuscany etc. You had, at least in

179

old world people's eyes, that other life – and threw it away. That takes some explaining.

Suddenly you have lost that exotic status in the eyes of people around you. The bells are tolling loudly for your out-of-the-ordinary existence. In fact, so loudly that you will have to explain time and again to others why you "gave up" your marvellous life abroad and returned like a beaten dog with the tale between its legs. It can be very difficult to get used to and is undoubtedly an essential reason to why re-integration is so difficult. The returner can be burdened by a nagging sense of having become a mere shadow of his former self. Many people who have returned to their old world do not feel appreciated. It is tricky to have to readjust to a life out of the quaint limelight that immigration provides. Expectations of other people's behaviour towards you must be readjusted; a painful process that left incomplete has the capacity to turn good men bitter.

Following on from the above, many returners often complain that coming back to the old world seem like such a retrograde step in spite the fact that going home is what they had saved up for and dreamed about all the years they have been away. A nagging sense of having slowed down, life in the slow lane, is not easy to rid yourself of. "I have bigger fish to fry" the returner will say (or think) dismissively without realising that smaller fish can be tasty and nourishing in a different way.

Old world pettiness
Small-mindedness is not specific to the old world though it clearly can be argued that some cultures have more of it than others. But pettiness so horrible that it deters you from getting on with your life, usually originates from the old world. The reason for the repulsiveness of old world pettiness is your extreme

sensitivity to this exact set of variation on the theme of pettiness. It once served as an important source of energy which made you emigrate in the first place. Your mind was fine-tuned into picking up any small sign of pettiness and making as much of a meal of them as possible for the sole purpose of stirring you sufficiently so that you would eventually have enough energy to break free of the chains of old world everyday life. The fine-tuning can rebound on your return to the old world and seriously interfere with your quality of life. You can laboriously learn not to focus excessively on the issues which under normal circumstances only impede on minor parts of your life. This overdeveloped ability to detect homegrown pettiness must however be included in the cost-benefit analysis of returning home - preferably carried out before you embark on the journey home.

Too many options
Throughout their lives the returners have been used to moving on to different places, seeing new people, tackling new challenges. Suddenly, they are back home were it all started. It can be difficult to settle – there seems to be too much choice. In many ways we are as a race happier with closure than with options. Options are exactly what the returner has. He knows things that old world people take for granted can be different and that there is another world out there where he can survive. His lost innocence cannot be recaptured. It is as if he had leapt over an invisible fence of insight from where there is no way back, a fence that from the other side looks more like wall. There are so many doors that he does not know which one to enter. Blinkers once lost cannot at will be put back in their old place. It can seem painful, but it should not be forgotten that the learned experiences allow you to see the world in a multi-

dimensional way that would not have been possible before you left.

Some immigrants have built their life around despising the new world people and customs and somehow made it the fundament of their life. No longer being able to hate so legitimately can be undermining. Life becomes bland. It is as if all meaning has been sucked out of you and into the jet engines that brought you back to the old world. Some distorted meaning can be regained by starting to despise the old world but it will never be the same as it is, quite literally, too close to home.

A slower pace

The pace will inevitably feel slower. This can be difficult to cope with because it allows you to take a look at things in yourself and your closest relatives that you did not have time to notice in the past. Long forgotten family frictions can easily re-emerge and an unfamiliar feeling of being trapped with these frictions may accompany the feeling.

A common trait in many emigrants is a relatively low threshold for tolerating conflict. Unlike people that have never moved much, emigrants know now that this particular place is not the only one in the world where they can make it. It gives an enormous freedom but less practice in dealing with chronic problems.

It must be remembered that the old world is not necessary a lesser world just because it is not new. Another long forgotten aspect of life is the joy of witnessing relationships and people developing without being in a rush to move on. This new slowness in your life provides you with an opportunity to face some difficult demons whose eventual demise may add to a different breadth to your personal growth from the travelling skills. This is a challenge every bit as demanding as emigrating and immigrating.

Loss of network
Loss of network is a testing experience especially for immigrants who have been away for a long period of time. It can seem real blow to find out that friends have moved on and family members have become old and frail. These features are most pronounced for retired returners who no longer have the workplace as a natural source for new friendships. Valuable relationships built up in the new world appear distant, and these friends can no longer just pop around to look after the cats while you are off for the weekend. It takes energy to meet new, old world people. It also takes energy to rebuild and expand on old, slightly rusty relationships. But fear not, the process will eventually yield more energy that it costs.

Envy
The most difficult problem that the returner will face is undoubtedly the little acknowledged and much tabooed human emotion of envy.

The great psychoanalyst Melanie Klein reminds us that envy is often based on a mistake; either an inability to accept our own failings, or the accomplishments of others, or the misapprehension that life ought to be fair. We envy those who have what we believe we should also have. Not achieving that, denigration is always ready to hand. An example of how closely the returner is policed for any signs of haughtiness is the way potential old world language difficulties are dealt with by people of the old world. Years of attempting to form thoughts in another language can lead to grammatical or phonetic mistakes in your mother tongue. It is not uncommon for envious people in the old world to pick up on this and treat the "perpetrator" with scorn and derision. Deep down, they would like themselves to have done what you did. The linguistic problems are too obvious a sign of the returner's years abroad, the immobility of the envious, and therefore consequently become a thorn in the side. Envy can unacknowledged be very destructive and function largely untroubled by any reason. Others may feel overtaken, belittled and humiliated by someone's achievements. This feeling of not having what others have – and ultimately believing that one has not lived as much as the envied - can become so unbearable that annihilation seems to the best way forward. This very primitive pattern can be difficult for the achiever to realise and may leave him despairing. Scorned lovers do not forgive easily.

A close cousin of envy is distrust. "Are you really sure that you did that?" can be a paralysing question interrupting your stories from your new world life. It immediately puts you on the back foot and quells your enthusiasm. But it does exactly what the question is supposed to do... "Don't get too carried away with your wild life over there. We can still queer your pitch by choosing not to believe you."

A female friend of mine described how her brothers and friends back home in her native Dutch town would continuously play down what she had done by moving away to another country and having an academic career. They would also suggest that nothing in her character had moved on since she left, constantly reminding her of things she was not good at before she left: "You are still the same good, old self that left 12 years ago. Moving on is not necessarily moving up!" This is a miserable travesty of immigrant life invented by people that had neither the courage nor the initiative to do it themselves. In other words, "you have not changed at all"… chiefly because we haven't, so you shouldn't either!

Envy stems from a mixture of fear being left behind, of not being good enough, and of fantasies about other people's lives being much better. Returning home either for visits and permanently can be a crash-course in how to deal with damaging envy. Envy can rear its ugly head in many other situations but when people have been out of sight for a while it becomes especially poignant. It is as if the fantasies run riot when we have nothing concrete on which to pin them. The envious are not entirely to blame. It is not unusual for returners to have a strong urge to justify why they have been away for so long. In order to make a good case for themselves, they do not linger too long on the difficult moments experienced while away. For people with envious predisposition this clearly draws up the battle lines and confrontation, or - what is worse – indifference, follows.

How to deal with envy
There is unfortunately no straightforward way of dealing with the issue of envy – which by the way is a concept that psychoanalysts have been struggling with for a century. Generally, the usual guidelines apply: be honest, be non-confrontational, forgive and realise that this may be more their problem than yours.

Pointing out too crudely that people are envious is a tricky business, because it usually sparks off an impenetrable defensiveness that can end lifelong friendships. Being aware of your own contribution to the situation can also calm the waters. It is not uncommon for immigrants to become so enthralled by their own fast life that they fail to recognise that others are also moving somewhere. Maybe not at the same pace, maybe not in the same direction, but still a movement that deserves recognition. So instead of saying something like "are you *still* here" when visiting old friends, it pays to look into other domains of their life and acknowledge what progress may have taken place. Yet, the best remedy for envy is for other people to get a real insight into your life abroad (achievements and failures), to have success of their own and to have not least a pinch of magnanimity. Relieving people from the basic anxiety that someone else's existence is paradise goes a long way.

Encounters with envy have the positive spin-off that you become acutely aware of the envy towards others when it appears in yourself. Turning things upside down can also be helpful and it is simultaneously a beautiful way of letting other people know that you paid a price by leaving them; in the worlds of the Dalai Lama: "Judge my success by what I had to give up to get it."

Quiet confidence
Overall, returning is for most a good experience in spite of the potential pitfalls outlined above. A strong feeling of having overcome challenges and being back home safely usually outweighs the problems. It is pleasurable to be regarded as an expert on a particular country and/or language. A quiet confidence that you have achieved something rather outstanding will remain with you well past the brief honeymoon period after just having returned home.

This confidence is supported by a feeling of having some intangible 'edge' in your contact with most people you meet back in the old world; a sense that you will be all right almost no matter what will happen – a sure sign of having, over a longer period, pushed back the frontiers of what seemed possible at the time, and survived it.

There will be a small group of returners who will continue to experience problems in the re-integration process. Saint-Exupery described himself as feeling most at home in "a remoteness beyond the possibility of homecoming". In his strive to achieve this state of mind he ended up at the bottom of the Mediterranean following one of his many dare-devil flights towards the end of the Second World War.

A useful antidote to returning home frustrations is to imagine the levels of frustrations you would have experienced had you never gone. Chances are that the thoughts of what might have been would have twisted your life considerably. Frustration is among the most toxic substances for the human soul.

A possible explanation as to why some returners get disturbed is that the problems they run into are largely unexpected. They are simply unprepared for any hindrances they may come up against, unlike when they originally emigrated and were ready for everything that might come their way. Some returners return to the old world expecting little else than eternal bliss and peace. It is not hard to imagine that that kind of naivety will create some disappointment. If you maintain your openness and remain sensitive to clues around you, there is no reason why returning home for good cannot become yet another successful integration-process from which you will emerge victorious because of your vast experience... and because you deep down are still one of them. The rules for returning are basically the same as for emigration with a fraction more emphasis on modesty in order to avoid stirring up too much envy.

Epilogue

Integration can be said to have happened when a satisfactory level of reconciliation between the old and the new world has taken place in the mind of the individual. I would argue that the most essential issue for the immigrant is to find an acceptable balance between accommodation (I change the world to match me) and assimilation (I change to match the world). The final outcome for all parties involved, at the very end of a long and complicated calculation, depends on just how right we got that balance.

Adaptation

Integration happens on many different levels whenever we enter a new phase of our lives - from moving house, to moving school, starting at new job, retiring to changing country. The problems are very similar but clearly of different intensity. The key to integrating successfully is the ability to adapt.

To adapt is comparable to the backhand stroke in the game of tennis. The more you practice the better you will get at it. The plasticity of the mind is amazing. Moving on can - like most good things - turn into an all-consuming passion that can get in the way of developing deeper relationships... which, it could be argued, also depends on some kind of integration skills. Few people obtain a fully bi-cultural state of mind, but you should aim to pick the pieces you like from each culture and mix them into your own idiosyncratic blend. You have thereby forever acquitted yourself from a life of normality.

There are those who fear that globalisation eventually will lead to a bland homogenization of culture and identity.

Many recent developments bear testimony to the fact that this process is being strongly opposed by an ingrained tendency in most societies to retain or even assert their ethnic identity (e.g. ex-Yugoslavia, the EU, declining fortunes of MacDonald's). We do not renounce on our cultural heritage without a fight, but clearly certain aspects of culture are in the longer run going to be more recognisable worldwide. It is not necessarily so much an occasion for tears as it one for doves of peace. This is underlined by the fact that cultural exportation can be very beneficial – in 1971 there were 30 democracies in the world, today there are 121.

Wealth

As I have accounted for above migration comes at a price: rootlessness, envy, loss of contact with loved ones etc., but on the whole it is a worthwhile enterprise that will leave us as richer and more insightful people and perhaps even societies wiser and more peaceful. Simultaneously, limitations have been brushed aside and you are now faced with real choice in the matter of how you want to compose the rest of your life. A greater sense of control has been achieved. If self-construction consists of the conglomerate of our experiences then there is little doubt that the construction you have made for yourself by emigrating is more varied and durable than would have been the case had you stayed behind. In terms of justifying their existence by being of value to others, immigrants are often accused of being extremely egocentric. While this may be the case in some instances things have to be seen in a bigger context. Your value to others over the longer term is also bound to rise as a result of a rapid increase in your knowledge and experience. And, by the way, nobody wants to live with someone who once had his plans seriously thwarted.

It is not uncommon when talking to old people that they will repeatedly tell you stories about their stay abroad decades before. The memories of the break away from the daily grind seem to trump all other experiences during a long life. To this day when I hear a New Zealand accent in a crowd a strong thrill still fills my stomach with pulses of spring-like joy and excitement, reminding me of my stay over 15 years ago in the beautiful country down under. The new world country obtains a very special place in your heart so that for the rest of your life your ears will prick up whenever something about this country is mentioned. It is not unlike having had a passionate affair and wanting to know how your ex-partner is getting on now. When it comes for you to evaluate your life, you can proudly look back on your time as an immigrant and ask yourself: "Where did it all go right?"

"Good morning, sir" said with a convincing English accent was the only sentence left in the repertoire of a 99-year old male, Danish patient I met in a Danish nursing home years ago. According to his relatives he had been working behind the allies' lines on the western front at the tail end of the First World War. As recognition for his contribution he had then been awarded a 2-year scholarship to become a shipbuilding engineer in London. By the time we met, his Alzheimer's disease had cleared the slate of absolutely everything other than the sentence mentioned above, which he would utter regardless of the time of day or the gender of his company. He was at that stage unable to recognise his wife, children or even his image in a mirror. It goes some way to show what his troubled mind had selected as the "edited highlights" of a life time.

A league of your own

The lessons learned and the speed with which you learned them cannot be matched by any other challenge you can put yourself through. Immigration is simply like adding fertilizer to personal growth. You have placed yourself in a league of your own. All it takes is an open mind, some degree of resilience and willingness to learn. No matter under what circumstances you might return to the old country, you will always maintain a cosmopolitan air about you that is worth more than any diploma. What you have experienced no power in the world can ever steal from you again. By straddling two cultures you have placed yourself at the juncture of two worlds, looking one way, then another. Cultural hybridization is as demanding as it is creative and emancipating. Learning to integrate is a passport to a larger land, a land of freedom and wisdom. Living abroad should be a part of the national curriculum. If it is true that we are the sum of our experiences then chances are that the immigrant life has added considerably to the final score. Have you ever heard about anybody that regretted having done it?